THE
ASTROLOGY
OF YOU

Unlocking love, creativity and
soul purpose in your birth chart

EMMA VIDGEN

Hardie Grant

BOOKS

Dedication

To my love and inspiration:
Matt, your Jupiterian generosity
and charisma know no bounds.

And to Plum and Sid,
who inspire me to be more
courageous every day.

Contents

Foreword

Astrology has a way of getting under your skin.

I was fortunate enough to grow up in a household where it was part of the vernacular. I loved watching astrology forecasts on morning television with my mother when I was a little girl, although neither of us could ever figure out how I could be such an untidy Virgo. Little did I know I was receiving my first astrology lesson: we are so much more than just our Sun sign. Nevertheless, there was always something magical about it. It made me feel like I was part of something bigger, and reassured me life was not unfolding in a completely random way.

Decades later, I began noticing certain themes playing out in my life on repeat. I felt a huge internal shift around who I was and what I cared about. It was like I was in the midst of downloading a new software update for myself. I was still me, but things had changed. I wanted to immerse myself in something completely, I was craving depth and meaning, healing and purpose. Intuitively I decided to investigate whether this season of uncertainty correlated with my birth chart, and unsurprisingly it did. The more I looked into it, the more it made sense.

A reading with a professional astrologer confirmed my suspicions. I was in the process of a major astrological software upgrade (my progressed Sun changed signs at the same time I had my Jupiter return). With nothing more to go on than the time, date and location of my birth, I listened in awe as the astrologer described what was going on in my internal landscape in fine, nuanced detail. As I was guided through my birth chart, astrology became an all-encompassing sensory experience. It was like visiting Paris for the first time after only ever seeing it in French films. The clunky one-size-fits-all approach of Sun sign astrology suddenly made way for my birth chart, a vivid, complex portrait of who I was. I was no longer an unusually untidy Virgo. I was my own special blend of every sign. I felt seen.

Inspired, I knew I had to learn how to read charts for myself. I was bitten by the bug, completely enamoured like someone who has just met 'The One' and won't shut up about it (sorry, friends and family!). I lived, breathed and dreamt astrology, literally lying awake at night thinking about planets, aspects and timing techniques. When I read charts, it feels like an almost sacred experience – a strange mix of déjà vu and effortless flow – the way people describe getting lost playing an instrument or painting.

Chris Brennan, from *The Astrology Podcast* (absolutely essential listening for anyone astro-curious), once said it's impossible to learn all there is to know about astrology. There are so many different philosophical approaches, so many different techniques, you never stop learning; it's one of the things I love most about it. For me, it is fluid, a practice that expands and contracts depending on where you're at in your life. The approach in this book draws on theory from different eras, from the ancient Hellenistic tradition practised by astrologers like Chris Brennan to modern evolutionary astrology pioneered by Steven Forrest. It's a special blend, a technique that I've found most supportive in my own life and in professional practice. For purists, mixing styles may seem downright blasphemous, but personally I'm OK with keeping things a little more fluid.

This book will give you a technical framework to understand the basics of your birth chart. To keep track of what's what, download the free worksheet PDFs designed to accompany this book by heading to **theastrologyofyou.com** or scanning the QR code on page 176. Journal prompts throughout this book are also designed to help you reflect on how the energies in your chart manifest in your own life.

More importantly, this book is designed to give you the practical tools to feel more empowered when you're moving through the world. It's my hope that after using my approach to unpack your chart, you'll feel less like someone to whom life just 'happens', and more like a powerful, vital participant with a unique array of gifts at your disposal. Most of all, I hope it gets you a little closer to accepting that every part of you is valid, meaningful and worthy of compassion.

Emma x

So what is a birth chart?

The very first thing you'll encounter once you graduate beyond your garden-variety horoscope is your birth chart (aka your natal chart or natal horoscope). It looks kind of overwhelming, and to begin with, it can be. But spend a little time learning the ins and outs and you will find that it's one of the most amazing tools you can master to live life with a sense of awareness, intention and curiosity.

Getting to know your astrological glyphs

You'll notice five symbols appear throughout the chapters of this book. You'll also spot them on your birth chart. They represent the primary energies explored in this book.

The Sun

The Moon

The Ascendant

The South Node

The North Node

What is astrology?

Astrology is the study of the relationship between celestial bodies (the planets, Sun, Moon) and events on Earth. Humans have been watching the heavens and noticing synergies between the sky and life on Earth for at least 3500 years. The earliest recorded birth chart dates back to 410 BCE.

◯ Your birth chart is a map

Your birth chart is like a picture of the sky from the moment you were born. It tells us exactly where the planets were (from the perspective of standing on Earth looking up, known as the 'geocentric perspective') when you came into the world. The position of the planets and the patterns they make – known as 'aspects' – weave an intricate tapestry of energy that describes everything from what you look for in a relationship to how you are with money. To cast your birth chart, you'll need to know where and when you were born. The more precise you can be with the time you were born, the more accurate your chart will be. You can visit **theastrologyofyou.com** to cast your chart.

◯ Your birth chart is an instruction manual for your life

Imagine how much easier things would be if you'd had a troubleshooting guide written *just for you*: a kind of go-to resource that shows you exactly what 'you do you' means. Well guess what, you've got it, and that cheat sheet is your birth chart. A birth chart is your very own personalised instruction manual. Understanding your chart can help you address recurrent patterns in your life, and consciously heal the emotional wounds causing them.

◯ Your birth chart is a mirror

A desire to be seen and acknowledged is a universal part of the human experience. Feeling 'seen' is one of the most common ways people describe the experience of learning about their birth chart. Your chart acts as a mirror to your personality and attitudes, with the position of the planets describing who you are, what you stand for and what you value. Seeing your reflection expressed in the sky brings a tremendous sense of validation, evokes a feeling of belonging and reminds us that we are all part of something much, much bigger.

◯ Your birth chart is multifaceted

One of the biggest revelations is realising that you have every zodiac sign somewhere in your chart. Don't like Virgos? Guess what: you've got Virgo in your chart, and the reason you don't like them is probably very clearly spelt out. Each one of us embodies the energy of each of the twelve signs in different ways. Those energies will be expressed in different areas of our lives, depending on which part of the chart (known as the 'houses') they fall into.

◯ Your birth chart is a tool for mindfulness

When you start to look into the mirror of astrology, you begin to develop an awareness of your inner landscape. You start to see your triggers and what you need to feel inspired, empowered and secure. You'll find clear indicators of the kind of karmic energy you carry into this lifetime, as well as what you came here to learn in the form of the Nodes. Some energy is going to feel super-uncomfortable, and often times this will be our greatest teacher.

Once you understand the magical, unique blend of energy that makes you YOU, moving through life gets a little bit easier. You learn how to play to your strengths, how to build relationships that will nourish your soul and how to ask the right questions when you're faced with a difficult decision. Your chart doesn't dictate your every move without any room for spontaneity, but it *will* give you a framework for what you need to consider when you're navigating tricky territory.

◯ Your birth chart is multiple choice

Looking at my own birth chart, you could argue that becoming an astrologer was inevitable. In actual fact, every one of my careers (astrologer, journalist, meditation teacher, even lawyer!) is reflected in my chart. One thing that's misunderstood about astrology is that it is a set-in-stone divination tool. While your chart conveys certain flavours of your personality and experience, what you do with them is up to you. This is how it's possible that twins are born with identical or near-identical charts but can go on to lead very different lives. Your chart is like an ingredient list in a recipe. It describes in exquisite detail a list of qualities especially gifted to you. What dish you decide to cook with them is entirely up to you. Yes, flour and eggs make pasta, but with a little extra sweetness they also make a cake – the choice is yours.

How to use this book

The astrological triage

Once you start experimenting, there's almost no limit to what you can do with astrology. You can use it to choose the best time to sign a contract (electional astrology), find where you lost your keys (horary astrology) or find the most supportive place to live (astrocartography). But the approach I find most useful is something I've nicknamed 'the astrological triage'. The triage approach involves assessing your life, and letting your concerns or symptoms guide you to a certain part of your birth chart for guidance.

When you're starting out, it's easy to get bogged down in the technicalities. The triage approach means you stay on track and remain focused on prioritising where you need help, rather than getting sidetracked with the theory and not actually applying it to your life.

The triage method helps you deepen your understanding of what it is you need to thrive. The birth chart is our own cosmic blueprint, and when you know how to read your own, troubleshooting issues in everyday life gets a whole lot easier.

You can use this practical approach for guidance on all sorts of issues – money, sex, work – but this book focuses on the four main topics I use most when working with clients.

01   Confidence, energy, creativity

      Look to the Sun for guidance on what lights you up.

02   Relationships, intimacy and love

      Look to the Moon for guidance on what makes you
      feel secure in relationships.

03   Self-awareness and interpersonal dynamics

      Look to the Ascendant for guidance on how other
      people perceive you.

04   Life purpose and direction

      Look to the Nodes for guidance on your karmic
      baggage and soul purpose.

Once you've found where your Sun, Moon, Ascendant and Nodes
are placed, read through the relevant parts of each chapter and
then use the journal prompts to explore how the energies manifest
in your own life.

You can also download worksheets designed to be used with this
book at **theastrologyofyou.com** or by scanning the QR code on
page 176. These will help deepen your understanding of your chart.

Then, use this book as a reference when you feel you need to do your
own little astrological triage. Check back in with the relevant section
when you need extra support or guidance on a particular area or
to deepen your understanding of other people. You can revisit the
journal prompts and worksheets and use them as a thought-starter
when you're feeling stuck or overwhelmed.

I

GETTING STARTED

Casting your chart

The first step to understanding your birth chart is to cast it! In the not-too-distant past, a professional astrologer would have calculated it by hand in painstaking detail. Now it's as simple as plugging your birth data into a website (such as **theastrologyofyou.com**) and voilà! All you need is your date of birth, your time of birth and your location of birth.

The time of birth is crucial as it directly dictates what sign was rising over the eastern horizon at the moment you were born (your rising sign/Ascendant). Depending on where you were born, the rising sign will change every couple of hours. It changes more quickly or more slowly depending on how close you are to the equator.

Your rising sign (aka the Ascendant) is not only a vital piece of astro info in its own right (more on the Ascendant in Part IV on page 116), but it also affects which signs occupy each of the twelve houses. Without the time of birth it's hard to get an accurate reading on your chart.

Your time of birth also impacts the placement of other planets. Your Moon sign is especially sensitive to your birth time as it changes every two and a half days, but the placement of other planets can also be impacted if you were born around the time they changed signs (known as when a planet 'ingresses'). The end of one sign and the start of another is known as the 'cusp'.

Help! I don't know what time I was born!

⊙ Finding out the time of your birth can be difficult and unfortunately, it really matters. Most birth certificates don't list it, although some hospitals may have a record of it in their archives. It may be an outside chance but it is worth a phone call or email to their records department. Here are some other tips to help you figure it out.

Ask your parents

Your first port of call should be anyone who was present at the birth or waiting at the hospital for news of your birth. Ask your parents what they remember. Was it light outside? Lots of babies are born around sunrise or sunset. If you get a steer around dusk or dawn, some weather websites list sunrise and sunset times going back decades and this could help you home in more accurately to your time of birth.

Dig for details

Drill them for any details you can. How soon after the birth did they call family members to share the news? If they had to wait for an acceptable time, maybe you were born overnight or very early in the morning.

Perhaps they remember the first meal they had after the birth – hospital food tends to be memorably awful – what they ate might help figure out whether it was close to breakfast, lunch or dinner.

Any detail around your arrival can help you reverse engineer the time. For instance, I had a friend whose mother couldn't remember the time but clearly remembered her father's favourite football team was playing in a stadium nearby. Her dad could hear the match from the hospital window when she was in labour. A bit of Googling helped work out what time games were played at that venue, and we could narrow down a window of a couple of hours. It wasn't an exact time, but it gave us something more accurate to work with.

Ask extended family

Extended family who were on hand – often roped in to look after older siblings – can sometimes be a more reliable source as they weren't in the weird liminal space that is labour. Ask them what they remember, where they were when they got the call or heard the news. Baby books, photo albums or birth announcements in the newspaper can also provide good intel.

When all else fails, call in the experts

If all else fails, cast your chart for midday and see what you get. If your Moon is towards the start or end of a sign (roughly the first or last ten degrees) it's possible it may fall within the next sign, depending on the time of your birth. Read both possible Moon descriptions in Part III (page 84) and see what feels right – one will almost always resonate more strongly than the other.

If you're really keen to get a better idea, you can book a consultation with a professional astrologer to have your chart rectified. Rectification is a process where the astrologer asks about the timing of defining life experiences (important relationships, changes to your financial situation, births, deaths, etc.) and cross-references them with the astrological transits that were taking place.

With enough information, the astrologer can make a very educated guess at when you might have been born. To find an astrologer who specialises in rectification, contact your local professional astrological association.

Why is having an accurate birth time so important?

☉ As little as a few minutes could change your Ascendant sign, which has a knock-on effect across your entire chart. In some cases, it can also change the sign of other planets and luminaries too, so it's definitely worth the effort to try and pin down the right time.

The anatomy of your chart

There are **four** key concepts to understanding your birth chart.

The **signs** are the different moods of your chart. Just as in life, we each have the ability to feel a full spectrum of different emotions, in our chart we carry the full spectrum of signs. See page 18 for more on the signs.

The **houses** are the different areas of your chart – such as your home life or career. They describe where to look when you want to delve into a certain topic. See page 28 for more on the houses. The sign occupying each house describes the mood in that area of your life.

The **planets** are your teammates, they offer support for – and sometimes challenge – the way you approach life. The sign they're in describes how they operate. The house they're in describes where they're most active. See page 36 for more on the planets.

The **aspects** are the dynamic between your teammates. They describe how well they play together. Understanding the dynamic helps recognise natural gifts and areas for development. See page 44 for more on the aspects.

The signs:
the colours
of your chart

Once you've cast your chart, you'll notice a bunch of symbols in the outer circle. These represent the signs – remember you have *every* sign in your chart, there are twelve signs and each sign is allocated thirty degrees (12 × 30° = 360°). Each sign represents your approach to or the mood in a particular area of your life. The twelve signs each have their own unique qualities, strengths and weaknesses, like different colours in an artist's palette. Just like colours, no sign is inherently bad or wrong, but like colours, we often have signs we prefer more than others.

To understand the different flavours of your chart, you need a basic understanding of what the signs represent. Some signs will play a more significant role than others depending on your chart. For example, the signs on the angles – at the start of the first, fourth, seventh and tenth houses (which represent your identity, your home/family, your intimate relationships and your career, respectively) – tend to play a more important role in your life. Thinking of your birth chart as a recipe for you, the signs on the angles are the most dominant flavours.

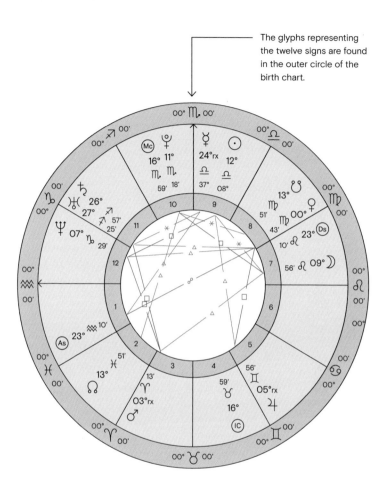

The glyphs representing the twelve signs are found in the outer circle of the birth chart.

Birth Chart Example

Natal
5 Oct 1988, Wed
2:22 pm AEST −10:00
Sydney, Australia

Aries

Ruling planet
Mars

Archetype
The warrior

Qualities
Aries energy is all about jumping in head first.
Fiery, direct and excitable, it has the courage and
tenacity to ignite action and take risks. It burns
bright and fast but can struggle to follow through.

Keywords
Impulsive, assertive, decisive

Taurus

Ruling planet
Venus

Archetype
The aesthete

Qualities
Taurus energy is steadfast in its commitment to
keeping things comfortable. As the most tactile
sign of the zodiac it has a flair for things that look/
feel/smell/sound good, but its attachment to
comfort means it can be resistant to change and
surprisingly single-minded.

Keywords
Calm, patient, sensual

Gemini

Ruling planet
Mercury

Archetype
The chameleon

Qualities
Gemini's superpower is its ability to be many
things at once. Its strength is an ability to stay
open to ambiguity. In its highest expression, it
makes for incredible communication, curiosity and
adaptability. When it is not functioning in a healthy
way it can feel untethered, anxious and indecisive.

Keywords
Complex, curious, eclectic

Cancer

Ruling planet
the Moon

Archetype
The nurturer

Qualities
Cancer energy is defined by its drive to nourish and care for the people (and objects and animals) it holds dearest. Highly sensitive and emotionally receptive, it draws its strength from vulnerability and an ability to withdraw. At its least functional, it is hypersensitive, stand-offish and defensive.

Keywords
Sensitive, empathic, romantic

Leo

Ruling planet
the Sun

Archetype
The rock star

Qualities
Leo energy is all about harnessing its creativity and sharing it with the world. It embodies a sense of personal sovereignty and is not afraid to say, 'Look at me!' At its best, it is generous, warm and surprisingly persistent; at its worst, it is self-involved, stubborn and overpowering.

Keywords
Social, individualistic, proud

Virgo

Ruling planet
Mercury

Archetype
The fixer

Qualities
Virgo energy is driven by a need for improvement. An analytical quality gives it the nous to look for the best possible way to do things. There is a selflessness that makes it incredibly generous but also prone to martyrdom.

Keywords
Discerning, considerate, refined

Libra

Ruling planet
Venus

Archetype
The mediator

Qualities
Libra energy is motivated by considered discourse, where everyone gets a say. It seeks balance and equality and has a strong sense of justice and what is right. At its best, it is insightful and thoughtful and at its worst, it can be antagonistic or co-dependent.

Keywords
Charismatic, observant, diplomatic

Scorpio

Ruling planet
Mars, Pluto

Archetype
The sleuth

Qualities
Scorpio energy is focused on digging below the surface – even when it's painful – to uncover what's really going on. It can be perceptive, sensitive and steadfast; at its worst, it can be paranoid, controlling and possessive.

Keywords
Perceptive, wilful, enigmatic

Sagittarius

Ruling planet
Jupiter

Archetype
The adventurer

Qualities
Sagittarius energy forges its own path, avoiding the mundane in search of something meaningful. At its best, it is brave, intrepid and has confidence in its conviction. At its worst, it is dogmatic, judgemental and afraid of commitment.

Keywords
Adventurous, direct, opinionated

Capricorn

Ruling planet
Saturn

Archetype
The rock

Qualities
Capricorn energy goes all-in on whatever it sets its mind to and won't let up until it reaches its goal. At its best, it is reliable and hard-working and at its worst, stand-offish and pessimistic.

Keywords
Determined, disciplined, capable

Aquarius

Ruling planet
Saturn, Uranus

Archetype
The innovator

Qualities
Aquarian energy is the ultimate visionary. Analytical, independent and resourceful, it strives for freedom and belonging. At its best, it is inventive and eccentric; at its worst, it is contrary and emotionally unavailable.

Keywords
Independent, analytical, original

Pisces

Ruling planet
Jupiter, Neptune

Archetype
The dreamer

Qualities
Pisces energy represents radical compassion, creativity and a sense of wonder. It is romantic, artistic and otherworldly. At its best, it is generous and creative; at its worst, it is impressionable and unreliable.

Keywords
Intuitive, generous, compassionate

All about elements and modes

⊙ Each of the signs can be further categorised by its element, (fire, earth, air or water) and its mode (cardinal, fixed or mutable). The elements and modes help expand on the relationships between each sign and its place in the astrological calendar.

The elements

There are four elements, each with its own qualities. Each sign belongs to an elemental family. Like siblings, the signs are all unique and different but share a common ground with their elemental brothers and sisters. Your chart may have a dominant elemental quality. You can check by tallying up how many planets are in each element. This is what it means when someone describes themselves as 'earthy' or 'watery'. We're often drawn to people who carry a lot of planets in the same element as our own chart.

Fire

Signs
Aries,
Leo,
Sagittarius

Common traits
Fire signs share a bias for action. They are driven and impulsive. Like a flame, they ignite situations and create warmth and excitement but can be unpredictable and reactive. As a family, they are concerned with participating, forward momentum and passion.

Keywords
Desire, excite, activate

Earth

Signs
Taurus,
Virgo,
Capricorn

Common traits
Earth signs share a talent for making things manifest in the material world. They are concerned with getting things done, and move through life with dedication, loyalty and commitment. As a family, they embody productivity, steadiness and resilience.

Keywords
Manifest, build, stabilise

Air

Signs
Gemini,
Libra,
Aquarius

Common traits
Air signs share a penchant for ideas and relationships. They are most commonly associated with communication and data. As a family, they're concerned with analysing, problem-solving and learning through connection with others.

Keywords
Rationalise, express, relate

Water

Signs
Cancer,
Scorpio,
Pisces

Common traits
Water signs are united by their emotional depth. They are associated with creativity, sensitivity and matters of the heart. As a family, they are synonymous with feelings, intuition and artistic expression.

Keywords
Care, feel, respond

The modes

Another way the signs are categorised is by the modes. The three modes relate to the part of the season (spring, summer, autumn, winter) in which each sign falls – the beginning (cardinal), the middle (fixed) and end (mutable). Signs that share the same mode will have common qualities despite being members of a different elemental family. You might notice you have a lot of friends who share the same mode as you, as well as some who share the same element. While you will be very different people, you'll have a familiar shorthand or approach to life.

Cardinal

Signs
Aries,
Cancer,
Libra,
Capricorn

Role
The initiators

Common traits
Each of the cardinal signs falls at the start of the four seasons. They are naturally more geared towards leading and big-picture roles. They demonstrate amazing initiative but can struggle to see things through to completion. Aries is the most active of all the cardinal signs. Cancer leads with the heart. Libra leads with the head. Capricorn leads with hands-on practicality.

Fixed

Signs
Taurus,
Leo,
Scorpio,
Aquarius

Role
The stayers

Common traits
Each of the fixed signs falls during the middle or height of the four seasons. They are the signs with the greatest endurance, which makes them both resilient and stubborn. Taurus embodies serious staying power, especially within the physical and material realms. Leo is persistent in its creative pursuits. Scorpio has a well of inner strength to persist with anything it truly cares about, while Aquarius is famously fixed in its ideas and beliefs.

Mutable

Signs
Gemini,
Virgo,
Sagittarius,
Pisces

Role
The adapters

Common traits
Each of the mutable signs falls during the final stages of the four seasons. They possess a more flexible quality. This manifests in different ways depending on the element – but always equates to a greater ease with change and letting go. For Gemini, it's a talent for collaborating with people. Virgo excels at pivoting to find practical solutions to problems. Sagittarius yearns for a change of scenery. While Pisces is a master at practising non-attachment to the material world.

The houses:
the compartments of your life

One of the most striking things about a birth chart is the way it's divided. You'll notice it's split into twelve sections, like twelve pieces of pie, with each piece numbered on the inner circle of the wheel.

The twelve sections are called 'houses' and represent different areas of your life.

If you think about your chart as your own personal instruction manual, each house represents a different chapter – your finances (second house), your sex life (fifth house), your friends (eleventh house) and so on.

If the concept of your chart as a map resonates more strongly with you, you can imagine that each house represents a different area of your life – your family (fourth house), your work (tenth house) etc. Planets within a house will add depth and detail to that part of your story and describe your natural strengths and challenges when it comes to that area.

Here's a brief rundown to get started.

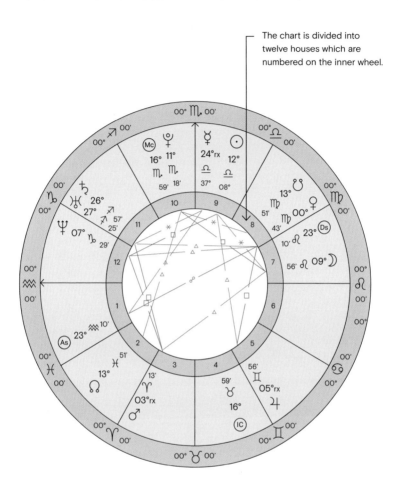

The chart is divided into twelve houses which are numbered on the inner wheel.

Birth Chart Example

Natal
5 Oct 1988, Wed
2:22 pm AEST –10:00
Sydney, Australia

The	**Key themes**
first	How you appear to other people, body, health,
house	appearance, identity, personal style

If your chart was a high-rise building, your first house would be what's on street level – it's the most visible parts of you, the parts that other people can see easily, just by walking past. It describes your appearance, your sense of style, and the way you move through the world. It also represents your health and body.

This is the part of your chart that helps you understand how other people perceive you, and the part to look at when you want to deepen your self-awareness. It's also inherently linked to your personality and will often resonate more than your Sun sign. That's because the sign that falls here is on the surface.

Whichever sign falls here will also be your Ascendant – turn to Part IV on page 116 for more detail about this part of your chart. Planets that fall in the first house will be especially prominent – think of them as being in the window of your shop front. Their qualities are clearly on display, easy for you to relate to and probably reflect how other people would describe you.

People who work with the body and appearance, such as personal trainers or beauty therapists, often have planets in the first house.

The	**Key themes**
second	Money, possessions, saving and spending
house	style, income

This part of your chart describes how you relate to money, especially the money you earn. Turn here to get a feel for your relationship to cash and your overall financial situation, as well as what you value and how you relate to material belongings.

People who work with luxury goods (such as cars or jewellery) often have planets in the second house.

The third house	**Key themes**
	Learning, writing, communications, speech, local travel, siblings, extended family, business, technology and your neighbourhood

This part of your chart describes early attitudes to learning (especially early years of school), writing and communication. It can also describe your relationship with your siblings and extended family, your sense of place within a neighbourhood and short-distance travel (think: within your town). Turn to this part of the chart if you want to deepen your understanding of your relationship with siblings or to delve into your strengths and challenges around learning and communication.

Teachers, writers and people who work with language (such as translators and speech pathologists) often have planets in the third house.

The fourth house	**Key themes**
	Family, home, childhood, ancestral lineage, parents, real estate

This part of your chart describes where you live, as well as where you've come from. It also reflects your childhood experiences and your ancestral story. Turn to this part to understand the family dynamics that made you who you are.

People who work in real estate, interiors or construction often have planets in the fourth house.

The	**Key themes**
fifth	Creativity, play, art, hook-ups, sex, pleasure, partying,
house	gambling, sport, children, fertility

This part of your chart is connected to artistic expression, individuality, fun and sex. Because it's all about bringing things into existence, it's also the section related to pregnancy, fertility and children. This is the place to look to understand how you have fun, and how you relate to your creativity.

Artists, creatives and people who work with (or have a lot of!) children often have planets in the fifth house.

The	**Key themes**
sixth	Work, routine, schedules, people you manage, pets,
house	wellness, organisational skills, illness, charity work

This is the part of your chart that covers how you relate to the grind of everyday life. It's about work in the 'bills to pay' kind of way rather than 'when I grow up' type career ambitions. It's also inherently connected to health and wellbeing. This is the place to look to get a sense of how well you handle hard work, how you cope with illness and how you take care of yourself. It also relates to being of service, people you manage and pets.

People who work in medical fields or service industries often have planets in the sixth house.

The	**Key themes**
seventh	Romantic relationships, best friends, business
house	partners, one-on-one consultative work

This area of your chart describes the people you're attracted to. Romantically it describes your 'type', as well as the kinds of characters who become best mates, confidants – even business partners. Here you will get a better understanding of the patterns and dynamics in your most intimate relationships.

People who work in one-on-one settings, such as counsellors and consultants, often have planets in the seventh house.

The eighth house	**Key themes** Shared assets and resources, inheritance, debt, tax, banking and financial matters, shadow work, trauma, power, intimacy issues, death

This area of your chart describes the parts of yourself you share – both materially and emotionally. It can relate to things like inheritance and family money, as well as any shared resources (think: cash, investments, property). It also reflects attitudes towards anything considered taboo or private like sexuality, control issues, intimacy and death.

People who work with other people's money (think: insurance and banking), or work with people who are recovering from trauma (such as therapists) often have planets in the eighth house.

The ninth house	**Key themes** Long-distance travel, foreign culture, spirituality, religion, higher education, teaching, media, law

This part of your chart describes your relationship to areas that expand your worldview such as overseas travel, media and even religion. It is also related to higher education, spirituality, the esoteric and law. Turn to this section of your chart to understand your willingness to open yourself up to new experiences, foreign cultures and learning opportunities.

People who work in media, law, spirituality, astrology or higher learning often have planets in the ninth house.

The tenth house	**Key themes**
	Career, ambition, reputation, public persona, fame

This part of your chart is synonymous with your career, professional ambitions and reputation. It's also connected to being seen and acknowledged, and even to fame. This is the place to look to see what's happening around your professional life trajectory.

People with a high profile or a desire for fame often have a lot of planets in the tenth house.

The eleventh house	**Key themes**
	Friends, workmates, community groups

This part of your chart describes friendships, the kinds of people and groups you're drawn to and the dynamic in those relationships. This is the place to look to understand your social self.

People who represent members of a community (e.g. politicians, advocates, unions) or whose livelihood is based on popularity (such as influencers) often have a lot of planets in the eleventh house.

The twelfth house	**Key themes**
	Solitude, escape, faraway places, the subconscious, dreams, fears, loss, surrender, transcendence

This part of your chart is all about your relationship to rest and solitude. It is also deeply connected to your subconscious and fears. This is the place to look to understand the parts of yourself you feel uncomfortable showing. Planets in the twelfth house may feel out of reach or fuel insecurities (e.g. the Sun in the twelfth house often manifests as a fear of not being seen or appreciated). People who work with parts of society who are unwell, excluded or displaced (think: hospitals, refuges, nursing homes, or even jails) often have a lot of planets in the twelfth house.

What are house systems?

⊙ Just as there are many ways to slice a cake, there are many ways to divide your chart. The different approaches are known as 'house systems'. When you cast your chart online, you might be asked to choose your preferred house system.

Some of the most commonly used are:
- Whole Sign Houses
- Placidus
- Equal House
- Porphyry

Which house system you use is a personal choice and one of the most hotly debated topics among professional astrologers. Entire books are devoted to the philosophy behind different house systems, but in the interests of getting started I recommend using Whole Sign Houses. This method is considered the oldest house system, and is most commonly associated with Hellenistic astrology.

It allocates thirty degrees to each house, with each house starting at zero degrees of that sign – including the first house, no matter how late in the sign the Ascendant (the exact degree that was rising over the horizon at the time of birth) falls. I believe it is the simplest approach and the easiest to navigate when you're starting out. I also find it to be the most useful in practice. If you like experimenting (I'm looking at you, Gemini), try casting your chart using different house systems and notice where the signs change houses. As you gain more experience, you'll likely find one house system 'fits' you best.

The planets:
your astrological teammates

When you look at your birth chart you'll notice a bunch of symbols inside the houses. These symbols represent the luminaries (the Sun and the Moon), the planets and the Nodes. Their placement shows where they were at the moment of your birth.

I like to think of these three groups as your planetary teammates. Just like at work, there will be people you get along with better than others, there will be members of your astrological team that you relate to easily, and others you find a little harder to handle. Understanding who they are and how to play to their strengths makes life much easier.

Their sign and house give you a steer on their personality (and how they perform their job). The shapes they make in relation to each other, known as 'aspects', add another level of detail and describes your team dynamic (more on this later – see page 44). Here's a rundown of who's who on your astrological team.

The glyphs representing the planets appear in the houses in the middle wheel of the chart. The numbers represent their placement by degree in that sign. The 'rx' symbol represents that the planet was retrograde.

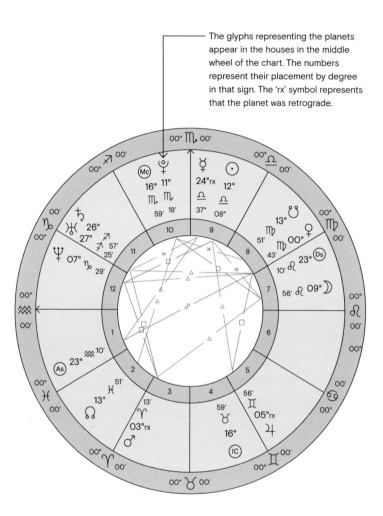

Birth Chart Example

Natal
5 Oct 1988, Wed
2:22 pm AEST –10:00
Sydney, Australia

The Sun

Job title
CCO
Chief
Confidence
Officer

Job description: The Sun's primary role is to bring vitality, creative inspiration and confidence. It represents the ego and helps you get comfortable with being seen, encouraging you to lean into your own sense of personal power. It's also associated with paternal energy/and or figures.

In aspect to another planet: The Sun brings a quality of luminosity and vitality in its aspect, elevating the other planet's significance and role in your chart.

The Moon

Job title
CEO
Chief
Emotions
Officer

Job description: The main job of the Moon is to help you process emotions. It describes how you process experiences on a subconscious level, your inner emotional landscape and what you need to feel loved, secure and nourished in relationships. It also describes how we like to receive love. It's also often associated with maternal energy/and or figures.

In aspect to another planet: The Moon internalises the qualities of the other planet, drawing the energy inwards and making that planet a key player in how you process feelings and express love.

Mercury

Job title
Head of
Communications

Job description: Mercury's role is to help you communicate and organise your thoughts, ideas and speech. It defines your cognitive approach to life and describes how you think, learn and express yourself as well as your natural aptitude for languages.

In aspect to another planet: Mercury brings a stimulating, psychological energy to the other planet involved in the aspect.

Venus

Job title
Head of
Recreation
and Aesthetics

Job description: Venus's role is to help you connect with pleasure. Venus describes how you experience desire – both in a physical and emotional sense – and how you relate to other people. It also describes what you value and your relationship to feminine energy both within yourself and socially.

In aspect to another planet: Venus brings sweetness and softness to aspects it makes with other planets, forging an energy that can be gentler, and more relationship focused.

Mars

Job title
Head of
Takeovers

Job description: Mars represents your drive, ambition and willingness to fight for what you want. Physical and primal, Mars invites you to get in touch with your competitive streak, own your sexuality and enjoy the fun of competition.

In aspect to another planet: Mars brings fire and assertiveness, like lighting a match under the other planet. Its desire for momentum and domination can see it enliven or overpower depending on the aspect and planet involved.

Jupiter

Job title
Head of
Growth
(Spiritual
and Material)

Job description: Jupiter's role is to help you find a sense of meaning and wisdom in life. It is about broadening your perspective – whether that's through spirituality, learning or travel. It is also connected to our attitude towards abundance, wealth and our ability to tap into optimism.

In aspect to another planet: Jupiter tends to expand and increase the significance and weight of a planet in aspect. It can imbue a sense of confidence in its abilities or bring an OTT vibe to the other planet's qualities.

Saturn

Job title
Head of
Quality
Control

Job description: Saturn's role in your chart is to help you take responsibility and achieve true mastery. It is about teaching you discipline, perseverance and grit. It's renowned for being serious and stern, but essential to ensuring things get done, and done properly.

In aspect to another planet: Saturn acts like a handbrake in aspect, slowing, shushing or even blocking the expression of the other planet. It can also manifest as restraint, casting doubt over your confidence to express the other planet's qualities. When it is making a supporting aspect to another planet, it can lend a sense of gravitas to its expression.

Uranus

Job title
Head of
Innovation

Job description: Uranus's role is to inspire a sense of rebellion, independence and innovation. Uranus wants to break all the rules, shake things up and help you embrace your own unique qualities. Wherever it falls in your chart will reflect a desire for freedom and individuality.

In aspect to another planet: Uranus brings an electrifying quality when it makes an aspect to another planet. It can bring a sense of instability, disruption, unpredictability or unbridled genius to the other planet's energy.

Neptune

Job title
Head of
Creative

Job description: Neptune's role is to help you relax, surrender and release control – whether that's resisting the urge to micromanage everything or getting lost in a creative process. It is a deeply artistic planet that inspires us to come to terms with the idea that in this life, control is an illusion.

In aspect to another planet: Neptune tends to dilute and blur the qualities of a planet in aspect. It can imbue the other planet with a sense of ambiguity, confusion or amp up its creative potential.

Pluto

Job title
Head of
Transformation

Job description: Pluto forces you to take control and face your fears. It shows you what you're most afraid of, and also where your greatest potential lies. Pluto reveals both your keys to transformation, and also where you are inclined to play it small and remain powerless. Much like Saturn, Pluto is probably not the teammate you want to get stuck next to at after-work drinks, but one that is essential to your planetary team and internal evolution.

In aspect to another planet: Pluto intensifies and magnifies the qualities of another planet. It accentuates the other planet's qualities, which may feel overpowering or even like a source of fear.

The Nodes explained

☉ Looking at your chart you'll also notice two glyphs that look like a horseshoe – one the right way up, one upside down. These represent the North and South Nodes of the Moon. They are points in space (as opposed to physical luminaries or planets) that represent your soul's path – where you've come from, and where you're going. Turn to Part V (page 134) for a deep dive into how to interpret your nodal story. Hard aspects to the Nodes represent a block or challenge they face in carrying out their job description. Soft aspects represent support they receive to help carry out their role with a little more ease. For more information on hard and soft aspects, turn to page 49.

The
South Node

Job description: The South Node represents your past life story and the karmic baggage you've brought into this lifetime. This baggage manifests as a kneejerk reaction that occurs when you're stressed, frightened or overwhelmed.

The
North Node

Job description: The North Node represents the lessons you've come here to learn in this lifetime. Its sign and house are always the opposite to the South Node. Embodying its qualities usually feels intimidating and unfamiliar but ultimately if you're brave enough to embrace them, it will be extremely rewarding.

Help! I have empty houses!

⊙ Look at your chart and you'll see that not all the twelve houses have planets in them. Don't stress! It just means no planets were in that sign at the moment you were born. That's not a bad omen; it doesn't even mean there's nothing going on in that realm of your life. You still have a sign ruling that house, and a planet ruling that sign, which reveals plenty of insight about you.

Advanced trick: identifying the managers of your departments

⊙ Each sign has a ruling planet, which I like to think of as the manager of the house it rules. If you're already comfortable with signs, houses and planets, you can check where the manager of each house is located to see what kind of 'work culture' they bring to that area.

For example, if Aries is in your first house, then Mars will be the manager of the first house (even if it's located elsewhere). Look to see where Mars falls in your chart and piece together the keywords for Mars's sign and house to understand the kind of culture it brings to your first house. For example, Mars in Libra in the seventh house ruling your first house means your shopfront (first house) is under management that is action-oriented (Mars), driven by a sense of fairness (Libra) and primarily concerned with developing strong one-on-one relationships (seventh house). Putting it all together, you come across (first house) as someone confident and willing to assert themselves, especially when it comes to maintaining fairness in close relationships.

For a list of signs and their ruling planets, turn to pages 20–23.

Planetary aspects: *your team dynamic*

'Aspects' are the patterns that luminaries, planets and the Nodes form with each other in your chart. When they form an aspect (when they are a specific geometric angle from each other), they become inherently linked. Aspects can occur between luminaries, planets and Nodes. Some angles or shapes make for a delicious new flavour – like tipping a bag of M&Ms into your popcorn – while others can be a little harder to balance – think chilli and chocolate. Looking at aspects adds another level of depth to your astrological vocabulary, helping flesh out the detail in your instruction manual.

To use the work analogy, imagine that aspects represent the social dynamic within your team and describe how your workmates get along. Some planets will play well together, others will clash. Conflict is inevitable, but learning how to navigate it or at least understanding how two teammates interact can make your work-life more manageable.

No need to get your protractor out to measure the angles on your chart. The chart generator highlights the aspects for you. They'll appear as connected lines through the middle of the chart and often in a table below as well. Depending on what branch of astrology you're practising, there are many different aspects, but the five traditional aspects outlined in this section are the most commonly used.

The aspects are represented by the lines through the middle of the chart.

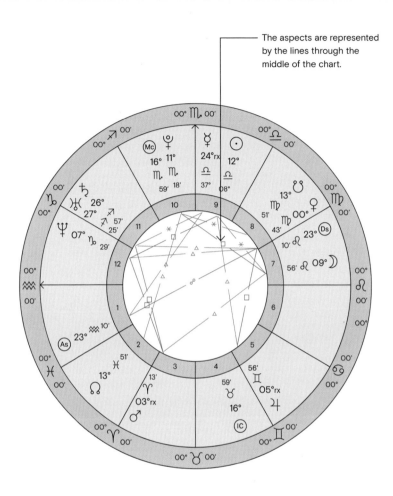

Birth Chart Example

Natal
5 Oct 1988, Wed
2:22 pm AEST –10:00
Sydney, Australia

Conjunctions

Keywords
merging,
blending,
unifying,
consolidating

This aspect occurs when two planets fall closely within the same sign and house.

What does it feel like?
The two energies blend together to create a new hybrid flavour that feels like a combination of both – as though two planets have had a baby, or you mixed a new hue from two different paint colours.

Make it work
The power of this new energy comes effortlessly to you. All you have to do is figure out what kinds of environments or relationships will work best with this new flavour combination. Depending on the qualities of the two planets, it can be harmonious and useful, quite unusual or even overpowering.

Sextiles

Keywords
attraction,
chemistry,
sparkle

This aspect occurs when two planets are around sixty degrees apart.

What does it feel like?
The two energies vibe off each other, creating a sparky rapport. Think of it as two very different flavours – like salt and caramel – coming together. Despite their differences, they complement each other. They taste better together as salted caramel than if you had a spoonful of one on its own.

Make it work
Concentrate on bringing an awareness to the spark between the planets and how it shows up in your life.

Trines

Keywords
ease, flow,
harmony

This aspect occurs when two planets are
120 degrees apart.

What does it feel like?
The two energies blend easily, think a classic flavour
pairing like fish and lemon. These energies work
together so well, they can be overlooked for more
interesting and distinct combinations.

Make it work
Just as you might not consider yourself a culinary
whiz for putting a wedge of lemon on a plate with
fish, the trine's energy can be so inherent to who
you are, that it gets overlooked. Actively pursuing
opportunities that showcase the natural harmony
of these planets is the key to success. Look at their
shared elemental characteristics (they are always the
same element) for a steer on how to make the most
of the energy.

Squares

Keywords
friction,
action,
activation

This aspect occurs when two planets are ninety
degrees apart.

What does it feel like?
The two energies clash in the most activating way
possible. Like two people who really know how to
push each other's buttons, neither one is willing to
compromise. This is not a simmering tension, but a
friction you can't ignore. The inner conflict evokes
a reaction and requires conscious work to integrate
or overcome. Because they are by nature very
activating and have a noticeable effect, squares
involving Venus or Jupiter can be a great asset.

Make it work

Try to appreciate both energies the same way a parent might strive to understand both sides of their children's argument. Giving each energy space to shine – the same way you'd give two bickering siblings a job they can 'own' and be proud of – is a productive way to handle the inherent tension. Consider their shared modality (they are always the same mode) for hints on how to find the best use of each energy.

Oppositions

Keywords
polarity,
indecision,
compromise

This aspect occurs when two planets are 180 degrees apart.

What does it feel like?

The two energies are at opposite ends of the energetic spectrum and feel totally at odds with each other. You may see-saw between the two approaches or feel stuck in the middle.

Make it work

Your challenge is to find a compromise and integrate the best qualities of both planets. Being conscious of their axis (see the Nodes section on pages 42–43 for more on the energetic axis between opposing signs) and working to find a middle ground is essential to getting the best from an opposition.

What makes an aspect?

☉ Because planets don't often make a perfect aspect (for instance, exactly 180 degrees apart to form an opposition), astrologers use a buffer on either side. This wiggle room is known as an 'orb'.

Different branches of astrology use different-sized orbs, and just like house systems, it's a hot topic within the profession. It's not uncommon for astrologers to use orbs as tight as two or three degrees or as large as ten degrees.

Again, just like house systems, personal choice and experience will help you develop your own opinion. In my own practice, I use an orb of up to five degrees for conjunctions – meaning the planets come within five degrees of each other in the chart – and seven degrees for the remaining aspects (sextiles, trines, squares and oppositions), meaning the aspect would form perfectly give or take seven degrees on either side.

What are hard and soft aspects?

☉ Squares and oppositions are known as hard aspects. Conjunctions, sextiles or trines are known as soft aspects. Hard aspects are more activating as the two planets challenge each other and fight to be heard or expressed.

That's not to say they are a lost cause; in fact, a hard aspect can yield more noticeable results if you work with it consciously. But just like balancing opposing flavours in a recipe you need to get the combination of energies just right to make sure one doesn't overpower the other.

In contrast, soft aspects blend the flavours of the planets involved effortlessly, creating a new recipe that just works. You don't have to do anything to get the benefits, the qualities are a part of who you are – often presenting as natural talents or capabilities (especially in the case of trines).

II

INSPIRE ME

UNDERSTANDING
YOUR SUN

If you're new to astrology, chances are your Sun sign is the one energy that feels familiar. It's the one you read when you look at your horoscope in a magazine, the one even most sceptics know about themselves.

It's not a coincidence the Sun is the most famous flavour in our birth chart. Being front and centre pretty much sums up what the Sun is all about. Stepping up, standing out and shining bright are all synonymous with big solar energy.

Aside from being the resident rock star, your Sun sign carries a whole lot of info about your personality, your worldview and, perhaps most importantly, what you need to feel inspired, creative, energised and confident. If you were born during the day the Sun is even more important.

When to use this section

Turn to this section whenever you're lacking energy, inspiration or confidence. Depending on your chart, you may be naturally drawn to people, situations and opportunities that feed your Sun. But some of us need to consciously work with its energy to get the best results.

Start honouring your Sun and you'll begin to feel a sense of lightness, luminosity and vitality – the kind of feeling people describe as 'living life in flow'.

When you're feeling invisible

The Sun helps you understand your relationship with the spotlight. This can be life-affirming if you've gone through life thinking there's something wrong because you just don't yearn to take the lead. We are not all born to be the lead singer of a band – and that's OK! But even the shyest among us have a happy place; a place where we come to life and truly shine. If you're trying to work out when and where you feel most comfortable being seen (even if you're an introvert) – your solar energy holds the key.

When you're feeling uninspired

Because the Sun describes your source of personal power and sovereignty, it's the number-one spot to look at when you're feeling lacklustre. Often, when we're feeling a bit *meh*, it's a simple fix: we've been filling our tanks with the wrong kind of fuel. By deepening your understanding of your Sun, you can figure out exactly what kind of energy your system needs to function at its optimum level.

When you want to fire up your creativity

One of the most magical functions of the Sun is its connection to creativity. We all have an ability and need to create, even if it wasn't nurtured in us as children. Connecting with your solar energy helps you understand your own special blend of creative magic. Just because you don't like drawing doesn't mean you aren't creative. Maybe your version of creativity is in how you declutter and organise your wardrobe (shout out to all the Virgo Suns in the sixth house!). Your Sun helps you reframe your relationship with creativity, and embrace practices that light you up on a soul level.

When you're lacking confidence

The Sun is connected to our relationship with swagger. Its sign, house and aspects show how much natural chutzpah we have, and the kinds of situations or activities that help feed our stores of motivation and ego. If confidence is an issue for you, nurturing your solar energy can be an effective way to boost your self-esteem and find your groove.

Illuminating motivations and perspectives: understanding other people's solar energy

⊙ Got a boss you just can't understand or a family member you cannot see eye-to-eye with? A look at their Sun sign can help understand the framework or lens they use to make sense of things. Because the Sun relates to our rational, egoic self, it's an excellent tool for understanding a person's worldview. Think of it as the light or filter through which a person views the world. This is why we are often drawn to, or just seem to 'get' other people who share the same Sun sign as us. Once you figure out the lens of their experiences, it's easier to understand their behaviour.

How to get the most out of this chapter

First, use the info in this chapter to fill out the 'Working with your Sun' worksheet available at **theastrologyofyou.com** or by scanning the QR code on page 176 to consolidate all the different qualities of your Sun (sign, house, element, mode, etc.) and dive deeper into how your solar energy manifests in your own life.

Next, use the journal prompts at the end of your Sun sign as a way to explore what you need to fuel your solar fire and bring more energy, creativity and vitality to your life.

The Sun through the houses

⊙ By looking at the house where your Sun is placed you'll add another layer of detail to help understand what you need to shine your light. For more about the houses turn to pages 28–35.

A first house Sun reflects a level of certainty about who you are. 'What you see is what you get' rings true. The way you see the world is consistent with the way people perceive you.

A second house Sun reflects that you see the world as a place where material security is important. You derive a sense of confidence and energy from building an independent source of personal capital – both emotionally and materially.

A third house Sun reflects that you see the world as a curious place to be explored. You derive a sense of confidence and energy from expressing yourself and learning from other people and experiences.

A fourth house Sun reflects that you see the world as a place to build your own sanctuary. Environments and relationships that feel like home nourish your sense of confidence and ease.

A fifth house Sun reflects that you see the world as a blank canvas. You blossom when you have a worthy outlet for your creativity and plenty of opportunities to loosen up and have fun.

A sixth house Sun reflects that you see the world as a place where hard work is an essential part of life. Your sense of confidence and energy increases with opportunities to dedicate yourself to your vocation, be of service and make a difference.

A seventh house Sun reflects that you see the world as a place improved by connection and partnership. You derive a sense of confidence and energy from opportunities to collaborate, learn through relationships and form strong one-on-one bonds professionally and personally.

An eighth house Sun reflects that you see the world as a complex and layered reality. Opportunities to go beneath the surface and understand things on a deeper level affirm your sense of confidence. You may tend to slip under the radar or feel uncomfortable in the spotlight. You may also be drawn to areas of life that are hidden or 'in the shadows'.

A ninth house Sun reflects that you see the world as a place to learn and discover. Travel, education or deepening your understanding of the world on a spiritual or philosophical level spark your sense of confidence and vitality.

A tenth house Sun reflects that you see the world as a place to achieve and be seen. You derive a sense of confidence and energy from reaching your goals, being out in the world and giving things a go – especially when you've got an audience.

An eleventh house Sun reflects that you approach life as a team sport. You derive a sense of confidence and energy from connections with friends, as well as feeling a sense of belonging, social acceptance and community.

A twelfth house Sun reflects that you see the world as a place of light and shadow. You could have a love/hate relationship with the spotlight, where a part of you yearns to be seen while another part finds attention overwhelming. This is a very common placement for celebrities and artists.

Planets in aspect to the Sun

☉ Looking at the aspects other planets make to your Sun develops your solar story in even greater detail. Here's a cheat sheet for decoding yours. Turn to page 36 for a reminder on what each of the planets represent in your chart.

Planets squaring the Sun ... bring a palpable friction to your solar energy. The qualities of the other planet electrify the attributes of your Sun, clashing with its energy and daring you to find a way to integrate both. Untamed, it can feel challenging and intense, but worked with consciously, it can be potent and prolific.

Planets opposing the Sun ... challenge the power of your Sun. The other planet's qualities will fight your Sun in a tug-of-war. You could find yourself flip-flopping between the energies or feel inherently split in your approach to life, depending on the situation. Your challenge is to find a middle ground between the two.

Planets conjunct the Sun ... fuse the qualities of the other planet with your solar energy. The Sun and the other planet mix together in a cosmic blender to create a new embodiment of your Sun – like your Sun has combined with the other planet to create a new flavour.

Planets trining the Sun ... bring a harmonious undertone to your solar energy. The qualities of the other planet will show up as a kind of gentle, effortless seasoning to your Sun. Think of it like tinted windows on a new car: nice to have, but you probably wouldn't notice if it was missing.

Planets sextiling your Sun ... bring a certain sparkle to your Sun. The mix is harmonious like a trine but has a little more punch – as the two planets have a more dynamic chemistry when they combine. It's nice to have (like a trine), but more noticeable and exciting. Using the new car analogy, think leather seats or a fancy stereo.

Sun in *Aries*

Driven by a desire to compete, win and take charge, this solar energy thrives on firsthand experiences. Don't worry about getting things perfect, just step aside and let an Aries Sun go first.

Primary energy source: Participation

The Sun in Aries is fuelled by a need to get involved. Standing by and watching while people get their hands dirty is a recipe for disaster. Being sidelined isn't just frustrating but downright debilitating. You need a seat at the table and an opportunity to get stuck in.

Personal perspective: Life is a competitive sport

For the Aries Sun, competitiveness comes from an innate need to improve on your own personal best. Sure, you'll read a lot about Aries needing to outrun *everyone* (and they do really like winning) but it's yourself (and your own personal best) you're truly focused on beating.

Creative inspiration: Blazing your own trail

Aries energy is not great at taking orders. Of course, that's not always practical in real life; there are some rules we kind of have to follow. However, when you're trying to get out of a creative slump, looking for ways to forge your own path is truly energising. Navigate an artistic roadblock by throwing out the rulebook and doing things your own way. Finding ways to foster a sense of independence is life-giving.

Confidence booster: Winning

If you're feeling flattened by a situation, schedule time to do something you're actively good at. Nothing cranks up the confidence levels of an Aries like getting high on their own supply. Reminding yourself of your own personal excellence in a certain realm will do wonders for your ego.

When you're feeling blah ... get moving

Even if you hate the idea of working out (yes, contrary to popular belief not all Aries live to train), physical movement will shift stagnant energy and stoke the yang energy essential for a happy Aries.

Journal prompts

Where am I able to feel in charge in my life?

Where in my life do I feel empowered to lead?

What activities or experiences make me feel genuinely excited to be alive?

What am I genuinely good at?

What am I most proud of?

How can I highlight these skills or achievements in my everyday life?

Sun in *Taurus*

Taurus Suns light up when they're surrounded by the things they find most beautiful. Building a life around their passion is the secret to unlocking true bliss.

Primary energy source: Comfort

With the Sun in Taurus, a life without pleasure is a life half-lived. That doesn't mean all Taureans need to drive a fancy car; but you do need to have space/time/means to indulge in your own source of personal joy.

Personal perspective: Easy does it

For the Taurus Sun, doing things in your own time is the recipe for good living. Whether you're booking a holiday or writing a song, what may look like plodding to everyone around you is just you doing things your own Taurean way. Like the bull, you cannot be forced. This is a sign synonymous with resilience and at times, stubbornness. From your perspective, life was never meant to be a race, so why rush?

Creative inspiration: Beauty

What isn't a creative inspiration to a Taurus Sun? This Venus-ruled sign sees beauty at every turn. Any kind of sensory experience will be an instant fire starter. Reignite your creative flame by immersing yourself in art or nature that truly moves you.

Confidence booster: Security

Feeling safe is a major motivator for Taurus energy. If you're worried by a decision, erring on the side of caution is the best approach. Surprises do not a happy Taurus maketh. If in doubt, play it safe.

When you're feeling blah … prioritise pleasure

Finding your thing – whether it's time in nature, foreign cinema or model trains (no judgement!) and making it a real priority in your life is an instant pick-me-up.

Journal prompts

Where in my life do I feel most creatively inspired?

How often do I make time to do the things that inspire me?

What people/places/activities make me *feel* good?

How safe and secure do I feel in my material world?

How can I build a sense of stability to feel more secure in my everyday life?

Sun in
Gemini

The Gemini Sun possesses an infectious kinetic energy that makes them genuinely interested in the world and intriguing to be around.

Primary energy source: Information

> Learning fuels the fires of Gemini Suns. Stimulation is essential. That could mean a stack of bedside reading or a long to-do list (or preferably both). While not all Geminis fit the stereotype of social butterfly/chatterbox, somewhere inside you there will be an inherent curiosity that makes you wonder (even if only in your mind), 'But why?'

Personal perspective: Why do I have to choose?

> Curiosity, contrast, multiplicity – these are the superpowers of the Gemini Sun. Hard to define and impossible to pigeonhole, Gemini Sun's ability to appreciate all sides of a story means you can play devil's advocate without being antagonistic.

Creative inspiration: Change

> The saying 'change is the only certainty in life' strikes fear into the heart of most people, but for Geminis, it's a dream come true. Any kind of variation – whether that's getting off the couch and going for a walk or considering an interstate move – is the secret to jump-starting your creative juices.

Confidence booster: Pivoting

Doing something that requires adaptability, analytical prowess and a willingness to try something different will boost your confidence. Finding a hobby or project that plays to your flexibility is a great pick-me-up. And if all else fails, try something new.

When you're feeling blah ... phone a friend

Gemini Sun's natural pep means they're often the glue that holds a group together. Reaching out and connecting when you're feeling off is the antidote to shaking off sluggishness. If you're not saying it, you're storing it, and that is not ideal for this Mercury-ruled sign.

Journal prompts

Where in my life do I have the freedom to switch things up?

Where can I introduce more flexibility or facilitate more change into my life?

How can I prioritise social connection in my everyday routine?

What have I always wanted to learn (but have never got around to)?

What big ideas keep me awake at night? How can I start exploring them?

Sun in *Cancer*

As a sign that's ruled by the Moon, stepping into the spotlight isn't always high on the agenda for Cancer Suns. Like the crab, they like to stay in their shell, but beneath their wary façade lies a sensitive and intuitive soul driven by a desire to love and give.

Primary energy source: Nourishment

The Cancer Sun is about feeding and feeling – often both literally and figuratively speaking. But that's not to say you yearn to cook for everyone you meet. One must *earn* the devotion of this Sun sign. Hell hath no frostiness like a Cancer crossed – 'crabby' is an adjective for a reason.

Personal perspective: You get what you give

Like the Moon, there's a responsive quality to Cancer energy. You have all the love to give, but not without some reciprocity. Because your loyalty knows no bounds, you expect the same, and aren't afraid to keep score (and feel disappointed) when people don't show up for you the way you show up for them.

Creative inspiration: Downtime

Cancer Suns tend to take on the energy of their surrounds which can be exhausting. Rest and time at home are essential to your general wellbeing. That doesn't mean you need to stay in seven nights a week, but a sense of familiarity can spark your creative flow. Prioritising balance between being out and staying home will help keep you inspired.

Confidence booster: Caring

It is through giving that you receive and through sharing that you are lit up. Nothing bolsters your confidence like the opportunity to care for something. Pets, people, plants, run-down houses – pick a TLC target and do your best work.

When you're feeling blah ... give yourself a break

Like the Moon, your luminosity ebbs and flows. It's OK if you're not 'on' all the time. Managing time and expectations accordingly will help prevent disappointment. The sooner you make peace with the fact that your energy levels tend to fluctuate, the better.

Journal prompts

What outlets do I have for compassion and nourishment in my life?

How much time do I devote to rest?

What times in my life did I feel safe/happy/loved? How can I integrate those memories into my creative process?

When do I feel most appreciated?

Sun in *Leo*

As its natural home (the Sun rules Leo), Sun-in-Leo energy doesn't hold back. Warm, generous and entertaining, other people can't help but feel brighter when they're in your orbit.

Primary energy source: Attention

It's a cliché because it's true: Leo Suns derive energy from being at the centre of things. Just like the Sun in our solar system, the experience of being smack bang in the middle, with others revolving around you, even if only for a moment, just *feels* good.

Personal perspective: I could do that!

Leo Suns see the world with a sense of potential. Joy and fun are there for the taking and you're brave enough to go after it, so why shouldn't it be yours? Your propensity to never say die can be both a superpower and a curse, making you unexpectedly reliable but also incredibly stubborn.

Creative inspiration: Self-expression

The opportunity to raise your voice and be heard/seen/read is all that's needed to get the Leo Sun's creative wheels turning. Putting something out there that's uniquely your own, whether it's a painting or a business pitch – and knowing it will be received by other people – will motivate you to try harder.

Confidence booster: Creativity

Sharing something with the world entirely of your own volition does wonders for the ego. Leos have the magic within to create; the key is to remind yourself of that magic and prioritise it often.

When you're feeling blah ... recalibrate your energy

Leo Suns can get caught up in other people's opinions of them. The simple act of calling your energy back to you (literally, stand in front of a mirror and say out loud, 'I call all my energy back to me') will help recalibrate.

Journal prompts

When do I feel most empowered to show up and be seen?

What outlets or environments make me feel inspired to stand out?

Where in my life do I prioritise creativity?

How can I make creativity a more important priority?

Sun in *Virgo*

Virgo Suns are turned on by the thrill of finding a solution. Can you fix it? With a Virgo Sun in your midst, the answer is always, 'Yes we can!'

Primary energy source: Problem-solving

> Virgo energy thrives on the opportunity to be useful. Whether it's helping a friend move house, streamlining a workflow or finding the most flattering pair of jeans, you get a kick out of researching and refining. When there is no scope to jump in and help someone else, you'll go to town with self-improvement projects.

Personal perspective: There's always room for improvement

> A drive to refine situations is a natural Virgo reflex. No sign is more productive than a functional Virgo Sun, but you can easily get carried away. Overworking is an occupational hazard. Being still, relaxing and accepting help can also feel deeply uncomfortable for you.

Creative inspiration: Editing

> For a Virgo, a blank sheet of paper is far more daunting than a messy manuscript; you do your best work when you've got something to work with. Whether it's a chaotic wardrobe or an impossible brief, unravelling and improving a situation until it's just right is a sure-fire creative turn-on.

Confidence booster: Helping

Helping someone else achieve a goal or improve on an outcome is a simple way to get your groove back. An act of service will play to your inherent altruistic streak and showcase your earthy practicality.

When you're feeling blah ... take a break

High expectations, a legendary work ethic and an overly analytical mind mean that rest is a Virgo Sun's greatest challenge. Since switching off and taking it easy are not in the Virgo vernacular, try approaching rest like a physical challenge. Schedule it in, research new ways to do it (such as different kinds of meditation, mindfulness apps or wellness retreats) and set yourself rest goals. It may sound crazy to other signs, but it's the best way to hold yourself accountable.

Journal prompts

When do I feel most useful?

What outlets do I have to help or improve the lives of others?

What areas or interests do I enjoy sorting or organising?

How can I incorporate these areas or outlets more into my everyday life?

What does my rest protocol look like? How can I refine my approach to rest?

Sun in *Libra*

When your Sun is in Libra, relationships are central to your experience. Whether it's falling in love, having close friends, being celebrated at work or all of the above, other people's feelings and opinions (about you) matter ... a lot.

Primary energy source: Connection

Libra Suns are a rare breed of unicorn who thrive on other people's energy. Not just a tight circle of ride-or-dies; Libra energy is genuinely lit up by the company of others – even people completely different to them. In fact, all the better if they're totally different. The illumination of seeing things from a different perspective is like catnip to this placement.

Personal perspective: What do YOU think?

You may not follow other people's advice (in fact you may seem to do the exact opposite), but you can count on a Libra Sun to seek a second opinion. Sussing out situations and reassessing relationships from *every* possible perspective is your signature move. A desire for equilibrium makes you a natural mediator, but you can also become fixated on exploring 'the other side of the story' to the point of being antagonistic or contrary.

Creative inspiration: Balance

As a natural-born aesthete, your proclivity for balance means you have a talent for arranging objects, items and schedules 'just so'. Whether it's a guest list, a holiday itinerary or the furniture in your living room, Libra Suns are masters of getting the mix just right.

Confidence booster: Interaction

Accepting a random invite, saying 'yes' to the left-field date or getting around to a long overdue catch-up will boost your confidence. Opportunities to work the room and vibe off other people's energy will have you feeling in flow in record time.

When you're feeling blah … insist on solitude

With so much focus on what's going on around them, it's easy for this Sun sign to feel confused, fragmented or overwhelmed by other people's opinions. Time alone may be uncomfortable but is essential to help you reconnect with your true needs, away from the white noise of other people.

Journal prompts

How do I prioritise social connection in my life?

What environments and relationships evoke a feeling of calm and equilibrium?

Where in my life do I get to explore ideas, places and people outside my own perspective?

If no one else's feelings were a consideration, what simple acts would bring me a sense of joy?

Sun in *Scorpio*

Scorpio Sun's strength lies in their powers of perception. This is a sign who doesn't miss a beat. Even when they seem like they're not paying attention ... they are.

Primary energy source: Control

Very few of us *like* feeling powerless, but for a Scorpio, maintaining a sense of autonomy is their life force. Whether it's a sense of agency over your work, health, love, or all of the above, personal power is key to a happy life.

Personal perspective: What's *really* going on?

This is a placement that is observant to a fault, making you both an excellent judge of character, a natural-born detective and sometimes a fervent conspiracy theorist. Part of this means you keep your cards firmly to your chest – a pretty good reason why people may say you're so hard to figure out. You're also naturally sceptical, gifted at diagnosis and magnificently strategic.

Creative inspiration: Depth

One thing is for certain: you will only feel creatively inspired if you're doing your thing with reckless abandon. Nothing will make a Scorpio Sun shrivel faster than a lack of depth. Just scratching the surface, brushing over details or doing things without passion just won't cut it for this Sun sign.

Confidence booster: Problem-solving

Tapping into those investigative powers and giving yourself a focus will feel great. Maybe it's as simple as figuring out why the Apple TV has stopped working or doing some digging into your ancestry. Find an opportunity to dig deeper and discover the truth behind a mystery that's piqued your interest.

When you're feeling blah ... surrender

As much as you like being in control, letting your guard down is essential to your wellbeing. When you're feeling tightly wound, a safe space and/or relationship where you feel you can come undone is a must-have.

Journal prompts

Where in my life do I feel safe to be truly honest?

Where and when (and with whom) do I feel safe to lose control?

What interests or passions do I wish I had more time to completely immerse myself in?

What areas of my life feel like they're lacking depth?

How can I bring a greater depth to these areas?

Sun in *Sagittarius*

There's something irresistibly charismatic about Sagittarius energy. They know what they like, they're confident in their opinion and they're almost always up for an adventure.

Primary energy source: Honesty

Sagittarian Suns need the space to do, be and express themselves without censorship. It's this freedom to share how you feel, what you want, and, most importantly, what you believe that keeps you feeling energised.

Personal perspective: In my opinion ...

What do you believe in? It's a tricky question most of us would need to think about, but a Sagittarius could almost always respond without hesitation. Not one to mince your words, Sagittarius Suns always have an opinion – even when you're not especially qualified.

Creative inspiration: Freedom

Working without strict parameters is integral to the creative process of the Sagittarian Sun. This is not a sign that does well being fenced in – literally or figuratively speaking. Engaging with opportunities where you're in the driver's seat and making your own way in the world is essential to staying artistically inspired.

Confidence booster: Being heard

This Fire sign loves to share their ideas – whether they're waxing lyrical about their favourite music or discussing their theories on international politics. Hanging out with someone who's happy to be a captive audience is a great way to get into the groove.

When you're feeling blah … try a change of scenery

The Sagittarian appetite for broader horizons manifests in quite a literal way. When you're feeling off, an escape from the everyday, even if it's just a mini-break an hour away from where you live, can act like an instant system reboot.

Journal prompts

When do I feel most free to express my opinions?

Who or what gets me fired up?

Where in my life do I feel limited or restrained from being myself?

How can I prioritise freedom and space in my everyday routine?

What opportunities or environments allow me to chart my own course?

Sun in
Capricorn

Goat by name, GOAT (Greatest Of All Time) by
nature, Capricorn Suns thrive on the opportunity
to achieve true mastery. Come Armageddon, find
yourself a Capricorn Sun and stay very close.

Primary energy source: Stability

Even the most carefree Capricorns thrive on a sense of stability.
Exactly what that means is different for everyone – maybe it's
a property portfolio, a solid relationship or a secure home.
Whatever it is for you, working towards a long-term goal – no
matter how humble – will keep your energy levels optimised.

Personal perspective: All good things take time

As a Saturn-ruled sign, Capricorns have a special affinity with
time. An appreciation for toil and legacy is innate to the way you
see the world and make sense of life. The desire to achieve and
leave a mark in some way runs deep, as does taking the long view.

Creative inspiration: Mastery

No sign aspires to GOAT energy like Capricorn – which is
perfectly appropriate given its symbol is the goat. Is it hard? Will
it take a long time? No problem. Capricorn Suns will be chipping
away long after the rest of us have given up and gone home.

Confidence booster: Taking the lead

Taking charge comes easily, but it's feeling capable that helps to fire up your confidence levels. Your natural ability to stay calm under pressure (even if deep down you have no idea what you're doing) is your superpower, and a shortcut to tapping into your self-worth. Negotiations, strategy or anything that requires extreme foresight will help you feel a sense of pride.

When you're feeling blah ... set a goal

Feeling rudderless is the biggest downer for Capricorn Suns. Setting and pursuing your goals, even for something trivial like a new personal best at the gym or learning a new beauty hack, will help revive flagging energy levels.

Journal prompts

Where in my life do I feel I am lacking direction or ambition?

What environments or relationships help me embrace a sense of responsibility?

What long-term projects have I got within my sights?

What activities or environments make me feel most capable?

Where do I see myself in five, ten, fifteen years from now? What can I do today to start moving towards those goals?

Sun in *Aquarius*

Analytical, individual and unwavering in their conviction, Aquarian Suns are a whole lot more than the eccentric genius archetype – although there's plenty of that, too.

Primary energy source: Independence

Aquarians often feel most alive when they're empowered to live life by their own rules. A natural flair for finding different perspectives fuels your need to do things your own way. There's a complex level of analysis that drives the Aquarian ego. You're able to identify problems on a macro level, and also envisage how to fix them.

Personal perspective: Standing on the outside, looking in

A sense of belonging is a central theme to your experience. Feeling excluded or outside but also craving a sense of connection, acceptance and community is a common framework for how you see the world. This paradox is part of the wonder and challenge of being Aquarian.

Creative inspiration: Authenticity

Despite their desire to belong, Aquarians get a kick out of doing things differently. Any kind of art, self-expression or professional opportunity to let your true nature shine gets your creative juices flowing. Likewise, being around people who are genuinely authentic and true to themselves will be a major creative turn-on.

Confidence booster: Innovation

Because Aquarians are naturally equipped to approach problems from a big-picture perspective, being given the opportunity to throw out the rulebook will be an instant mood booster. Look for opportunities to experiment or go out on a limb. If in doubt, keep it weird.

When you're feeling blah ... find your people

Nothing lights up an Aquarian Sun like being in the company of like-minded people. Whether it's a music festival, an online forum or a charity organisation, feeling part of something bigger is a great way to find a sense of lightness and connect to your joy.

Journal prompts

When do I feel safest to be myself?

Who do I feel most connected to on an ideological level?

How can I strengthen my relationship to community?

What makes me truly unique? How can I showcase this part of myself in my everyday life?

Where do I feel most accepted?

Sun in *Pisces*

While creativity runs deep, there is so much more to Piscean Suns. Compassion, intuition and a desire to merge with something meaningful are at the heart of their energy.

Primary energy source: Surrender

A profound urge to transcend, escape, and above all else, give yourself over wholly and fully to something – whether it's love, work or art – is the common thread to all Pisces energy. Yours is a sign that yearns to get lost in the process. The end result is a secondary concern. Finding outlets worthy of your passion and vision is your biggest challenge.

Personal perspective: Transcending the everyday

As a Jupiter-ruled sign, Pisces people see the world beyond the everyday. Both in a practical sense and a more philosophical context, trying to sort and label experiences, people or places is of little interest. The universe is a vast place filled with possibilities and magic; organising things is a waste of time that could have been spent on more meaningful pursuits.

Creative inspiration: Meaning

Seeking out ways to find magic in the mundane is key. Slowing down and giving yourself the opportunity to mine the deeper wisdom from experiences – even the seemingly boring, everyday moments – will help kickstart your creative inspiration.

Confidence booster: Love

Because Piscean Suns love to give themselves over wholly to things they care about – jobs, relationships, projects – nothing peps them up like feeling they can go all-in. Arguably no other sign needs to find what they love, and do it every day as much as the Piscean sun.

When you're feeling blah ... rest

The penchant for giving yourself over completely to things means your risk of burnout is high. Forcing yourself to take a break – not just physically but also emotionally – is important. You can't pour from an empty cup.

Journal prompts

Where in my life do I feel free to immerse myself completely?

When do I feel a connection to something more meaningful?

What do I daydream about most often? How can I integrate that into my everyday reality?

Where and when do I feel free to express my creativity without boundaries?

How often can I let go and escape the everyday with something, or someone, I care about?

III

NURTURE ME

UNDERSTANDING YOUR MOON

Dip a toe into the astrology of relationships and Google will tell you it's all about Venus. And while Venus does describe how you relate to other people and what brings you pleasure, I believe it's the Moon that offers the strongest romantic intel. Your Moon sign reveals your most visceral love language. It is how you 'do' love before you utter a single word or lay a finger on another person. For this reason, the Moon holds the most potential for helping transform your relationships.

Your Moon sign helps shine the light of awareness on what you *need* as opposed to what you *want* (which is Venus territory) in a relationship. You might chase the social media–hating, emotionally unavailable human island, but what you actually *need* is the foot-in-mouth, adorable person who will eat pizza in bed while you watch *Friends* re-runs all weekend. Once you understand what it is your Moon needs in order to feel good, you can start to make more conscious relationship decisions.

If you're in a relationship, the Moon can be super-helpful too. The snap, crackle and pop of your initial attraction is connected to Mars and Venus. But it's the Moon that really speaks to what you need to maintain a sense of love and security within the relationship. If you're born at night, your moon will have a more significant influence in your chart.

When to use this section

Turn to this section whenever you're feeling stressed, anxious or confused about any of your close relationships. While it's written with a focus on romantic attachment, your Moon also translates to your closest bonds with friends and family.

Even if you're simply curious about your relationship style or keen to strengthen your connection with the most important people in your life, understanding your Moon sign will be incredibly rewarding.

You keep running into the same relationship problems

If you've noticed you keep having the same argument with your partner, this section should be your first port of call. Understanding our unconscious emotional response to people or situations is a powerful step in addressing what's really going on beneath the surface and getting to the root cause of the problem.

You feel like you're speaking a different language to your partner

If you crave epic declarations of love but your partner just can't seem to take the hint, have a look at your Moon signs. The intuitive, unspoken nature of Moon energy means we often aren't aware of the way we seek and show our love. Once we start to understand how our partner 'does' love and what they need to feel safe, it's much easier to appreciate and reciprocate their own special love language.

You're ready to meet someone

Reinstalling an app or setting up a new profile? Before you hit 'save', take a look at your Moon. Realising what it is that you actually need to feel secure in a relationship is like being handed a missing piece to your romantic puzzle. With an awareness of your Moon, you begin to appreciate what kind of person will understand and meet your needs, so you can make more informed romantic choices.

You keep falling for the same type

If you're frustrated that you keep winding up with the same kind of (wrong) person, a deep dive into your Moon sign can be enlightening. Because our Moon operates below the surface, when we put ourselves out there – especially online – we tend not to express our instinctive, subliminal yearning. Instead, it's what we think we should be saying or what we think we want (again, this is Venus territory).

How to get the most out of this chapter

First, use the info in this chapter to fill out the 'Working with your Moon' worksheet available for download at **theastrologyofyou.com** or by scanning the QR code on page 176 to consolidate all the different qualities of your Moon (sign, house, element, mode) and dive deeper into how it's expressed in your chart.

Next, use the journal prompts at the end of your Moon sign to explore what you need to improve your relationships.

The Moon through the houses

☽ The house where your Moon is placed adds another layer of detail to understanding how you process your emotions and express love.

The Moon in the first house reflects a tendency to wear your heart on your sleeve. Your emotional response runs close to the surface making you something of an open book, easily read by those around you.

The Moon in the second house shows a tendency to express your love through material means. You may love giving gifts and feel most nourished when you have the financial freedom to spoil the people you care about.

The Moon in the third house is nourished by relationships where communication reigns supreme. You may be drawn to relationships where banter is essential and/or feel most fulfilled by connections where you both articulate your feelings freely.

The Moon in the fourth house is nourished by feeling a sense of security behind doors, and may yearn for domestic bliss. You may have an especially strong relationship with your parents or dream of building a tight family unit of your own. You are nourished by time away from the spotlight.

The Moon in the fifth house feels most secure when it's given the opportunity to be creative and playful. You could be emotionally sated by art, music or sport. As the house that rules children, you may also have a natural ease around them, and/or a strong desire for kids of your own.

The Moon in the sixth house feels nourished when it has an opportunity to give of itself. Caring for other people and generally feeling busy, needed and responsible is what makes you feel emotionally sated.

The Moon in the seventh house is happiest when it is in communion with another person. Forming strong intimate relationships – romantically and platonically – is important for developing your sense of security. You may even consider yourself a serial monogamist.

The Moon in the eighth house can reflect someone who is a little hard to reach emotionally – at least initially. When you do let your guard down, you may be drawn to intense, cathartic, emotional experiences.

The Moon in the ninth house is nourished by opportunities and relationships that expand your horizons. Relationships that feel like an adventure and open you up to new perspectives will feel the most nourishing to you.

The Moon in the tenth house thrives on experiences to develop and grow in the world. You may be in love with your career, fall in love at work, or be drawn to relationships that garner admiration and attention from other people.

The Moon in the eleventh house blossoms in relationships where they feel they are loved and respected not only as a lover, but as a friend. Social connection is essential to help you develop a secure attachment.

The Moon in the twelfth house feels safest when it has a degree of independence. You might seem a little detached or thrive in relationships where you are afforded space and freedom to do your own thing.

Planets in aspect to the Moon

Planets in hard aspect to the Moon (square or opposition) can bring a layer of complexity to the Moon's natural qualities and challenge your ability to express yourself emotionally. They can make it harder for you to be forthcoming with your feelings (especially when the other planet is Saturn), create a greater sense of reactivity or volatility (especially when the other planet is Mars) or intensify the Moon's emotional response (when the other planet is Jupiter or Pluto).

Planets conjunct the Moon fuse the characteristics of the other planet to it. Depending on the combination, the new mix can amp up the Moon's sensitivity (when conjunct Jupiter or Venus, for instance) or toughen it up (when conjunct a fierce planet like Saturn, Pluto or Mars).

Planets in supporting aspects (trines or sextiles) to the Moon offer a helping hand to express your Moon. They can add ease (trines) or a sparkly chemistry (sextiles) to the way you embody your Moon.

Moon in *Aries*

The freedom to be impulsive and fun motivates an Aries Moon. Arguably the most physical of all lunar signs, explosive attraction is a non-negotiable, as is a partner who lets them take the lead – at least some of the time.

Relationship needs: Chemistry

Aries Moons want and *need* to get physical. Teaming up with someone whose energy levels are a match for yours – not just sexually, but for life in general – is essential. Above all else, confidence and courage stoke the fires of desire. A partner unafraid to take risks and who trusts you enough to follow you into battle (even if it's simply backing you up in an argument at a dinner party) makes a great match.

Deepen your bond by ... asking your partner to get more comfortable with confrontation

This is not a lunar sign that can hold in their feelings. Got something on your mind? Spit it out! Finding ways to discuss what's bothering you will not only improve the relationship but also bring a fiery spark that will be a serious turn-on.

Greatest fear: Sharing

A natural sense of independence means Aries Moons not only need their own space but can feel suffocated easily. Sharing –

whether it's a drawer in the bathroom or how you're *really* feeling – can be tricky. Let your partner know it's a pressure point, and ask them to be patient.

Relationship roadblocks

Dating: Directness

The danger of foot-in-mouth is real. The directness and decisiveness of the Moon in Aries can be exhilarating at its best, but abrupt at its worst. Be mindful that before someone gets to know you, your frankness can be intimidating.

Relationships: Neediness

Nothing turns an Aries Moon off faster than a partner who seems co-dependent. Because you're generally self-sufficient, the faintest whiff of neediness can spook you. Remember your independence is a gift but not everyone is as autonomous as you.

Journal prompts

How can I bring a sense of excitement and spontaneity to my relationship?

Do I look for partners who let me take the lead with decision-making at least some of the time?

Is my relationship secure enough to explore healthy confrontation? How can I nurture this dynamic?

How can I show more sensitivity to my partner's or potential partner's feelings and needs? How are they different to my own?

Moon in *Taurus*

Sensual and loyal, people with the Moon in Taurus tend to be happiest when they're doing what they've always done. Routine, ease and lack of resistance nourish their soul. The most embodied of all the Earth signs, a Taurean Moon values connection and pleasure.

Relationship needs: Feeling valued

As a Venus-ruled moon sign, finding a partner who makes you feel truly valued is a non-negotiable. Whether it's words, deeds or gifts (or all of the above!) regular reminders of how they feel about you is an essential ingredient for a happy relationship.

Deepen your bond by ... asking your partner to indulge your senses

Moon in Taurus people have a penchant for anything that *feels* good. This makes you a naturally indulgent partner who loves to spoil and be spoiled. Slow down and take it easy, spend the whole day in bed; why have a quickie when you could make a day – or a weekend – of it?

Greatest fear: Change

Someone looking for a partner who sees uncertainty as an exciting potential, and chaos as an exhilarating challenge, may struggle with a Taurus Moon. A partner who understands your resistance to change and has the patience to know when to plant the seed (hint: EARLY) and let you warm to an idea slowly and on your own terms, will support your needs best.

Relationship roadblocks

Dating: Compromise

Your low-key chill may come across as easygoing, but you like to do things in your own time. A hook-up who tries to get serious faster than you're ready will learn firsthand just how stubborn you can be.

Relationships: Evolving

An aversion to change means Taurean Moons can hold on to things – relationships included – long beyond their use-by date. In love, your unwillingness to yield – especially when it comes to taking a risk or trying something different – can be your undoing. Try to remember that compromise is essential to a happy partnership.

Journal prompts

How does my partner react to my need to come to things in my own time?

What rituals or routines help me feel safe in relationships?

What sensory experiences help me connect with my sexuality?

What simple, nonverbal acts make me feel more valued and loved in relationships?

Moon in *Gemini*

Laughter is the preferred foreplay for this Moon sign, that's instinctively drawn to intellectual connections. But don't be fooled into thinking brains = boring, this is a placement that finds nothing *less* sexy than someone who takes themselves too seriously.

Relationship needs: Banter

> Above all else, Gemini Moons need really good chat from their partner. That doesn't mean you have to be with someone who has the same ideas or opinions as you – you're probably more intrigued by someone who is your polar opposite. So long as your partner can keep up with your intellectual dynamism and isn't afraid of a little bit of friendly debate, they'll do just fine.

Deepen your bond by ... asking your partner to prioritise fun

> Gemini Moons love to laugh, play and learn. Finding ways to connect that crack you up will be a major aphrodisiac for all involved. Explore ways to fall more in love with each other as people and friends – not just lovers.

Greatest fear: Emotion

> The mercurial energy of a Gemini Moon can often see this lunar placement acting from their head rather than their heart. Being lost in thought makes coming back to your body and expressing your feelings or vulnerability difficult.

Relationship roadblocks

Dating: Indecision

Your charismatic and kinetic energy means dating comes naturally, but an innate tendency towards indecision can manifest as flakiness. At its least functional, a Gemini Moon's disconnect from the emotional impact of your words can make you seem fickle or insensitive.

Relationships: Levity

Your ability to sidestep the elephant in the room is the stuff of legends. Your desire for keeping things fun means you often shy away from heavy but necessary conversations. Making jokes at inappropriate times or playing down the emotional weight of a situation are common (sometimes tone-deaf) ways you manage your discomfort with tricky emotional terrain.

Journal prompts

Do I choose partners who make me laugh?

What interests or activities do we *both* find fun and stimulating?

Do I feel safe to share what's on my mind even when it's completely inappropriate?

How can I show my partner with my words and actions how seriously I value our relationship?

Moon in *Cancer*

The Moon is both soft and strong placed in Cancer – the sign it rules. In love, Cancer Moons need a deep, nourishing emotional bond. This is not a placement who simply falls into step with someone on an intellectual level or out of convenience; there must be a powerful emotional resonance.

Relationship needs: Commitment

It was no doubt a Cancer who came up with the concept of a soul mate. Romance and emotional candour are imperatives. On a base level, Cancerian energy seeks security and sanctuary. In love, the Cancer Moon needs a relationship where the full spectrum of emotions flows freely. A partner with the emotional maturity to honour your emotions is non-negotiable. Someone who will be there and hold space no matter how you're feeling.

Deepen your bond by ... asking your partner to document your relationship

Cancerian energy is wildly sentimental. Photo albums, playlists, love letters, anything that shows they were paying attention at a pivotal moment, will strike a chord.

Greatest fear: A loveless partnership

Believe it or not, there are people who stay together for reasons *other* than being in love (think: convenience, apathy), but you can

bet they don't have a Cancer Moon. You need serious intimacy
and romance and an emotional connection that is deep
and heartfelt.

Relationship roadblocks

Dating: Rushing things

A tendency to give yourself over wholly to the experience of
falling in love can obscure red flags. Cancerians can fall hard and
fast, with an 'I can fix them' approach that makes casual hook-ups
feel empty.

Relationships: Carer's fatigue

The receptive nature of a Cancer Moon means you'll carry
other people's emotional baggage more than other signs.
This tendency to embody the role of the carer can leave you
feeling bereft, resentful and unappreciated. Make sure your
own emotional energy reserves are full before you rush to
the aid of those around you.

Journal prompts

How comfortable do I feel sharing my deepest emotions
with my partner?

How does my partner respond when I cry?

When do I feel taken for granted?

When do I find myself in relationships where I play out
a parent–child dynamic?

How can I prioritise more romance in my daily life?

Moon in *Leo*

Notice me. Watch me. Admire me. Leo Moons have so much love to give, so long as they're given centre stage to share it from. Their love is playful, loyal and abundant, but speaking up when they need support doesn't come easily.

Relationship needs: Appreciation

> Even the most demure lunar Leos need to feel the heat of their lover's gaze. The power of a genuine compliment or a heartfelt 'thank you' goes a long way with you. Your generosity knows no bounds too, so long as there is sincere acknowledgement and gratitude for what you give.

Deepen your bond by … asking your partner to get creative

> Creativity runs deep, although it is not always immediately obvious. Finding a partner who makes you feel safe to express your artistic side will help deepen your connection.

Greatest fear: Vulnerability

> Your Leo pride makes it especially hard to ask for what you want. Finding playful ways to express your needs will help love run more smoothly. A partner who can see through your lion-hearted façade and facilitates open communication will help you open up and show your vulnerable side when you're feeling sensitive.

Relationship roadblocks

Dating: Pride

The excitement of casual hook-ups is all good fun, so long as *you're* the one playing the field. When the boot is on the other foot, sharing the spotlight with another person is crushing. Expect 'dump or be dumped' mode to be activated at the slightest sign of sharing someone's attention.

Relationships: Stubbornness

One of the greatest qualities (and most frustrating traits) of a Leo Moon is its unshakable consistency. As a fixed sign you're prone to stubbornness. Add your propensity for pride into the mix and you make a formidable opponent and a reluctant abdicator.

Journal prompts

Where am I afraid to show my vulnerability?

What would make me feel safer to share my hopes, dreams and fears with my partner?

When do I feel genuinely desired by my partner?

How do I like my partner to show gratitude?

Moon in *Virgo*

When the Moon is in Virgo, it expresses its love through acts of service. A desire to find best practice in all they do means they're never *not* analysing how to improve and refine things – including their relationship.

Relationship needs: Understanding

> Like all Virgo placements, the Moon in Virgo likes to be put to work. In love, you enjoy healthy opportunities to take care of your partners. Being with someone who understands that your love language errs on the side of practical (rather than whimsical) and adores you for it, is essential.

Deepen your bond by ... asking your partner to articulate their gratitude

> Chances are, you're performing tiny acts of devotion (albeit, potentially mundane) on a daily basis. Having a partner show that they have not only noticed but they truly appreciate your hard work will make your heart soar.

Greatest fear: Not measuring up

> More angsty than emotional, an unchecked Virgo Moon can worry incessantly about not being good enough. A partner who can hold space for your anxiety will feel like home. It can be useful to explain that plenty of unprompted, verbal reassurance will help head off your inner critic.

Relationship roadblocks

Dating: Fussiness

Your relentless pursuit of perfection can make you tough on potential partners. Dismissing people for small missteps early on in the relationship is often a signature move. Try to be a little bit forgiving, remember we are only human.

Relationships: Practicality

Your pragmatism can be misunderstood as a complete lack of romantic imagination. The truth is no sign can be quite as romantic. Instead of buying flowers, you'll find the most effective compost for planting a rose bush outside your partner's window for year-round blooms.

Journal prompts

When am I scared of not being good enough in relationships?

Does my partner understand and appreciate the way I express my love and devotion?

Do I feel safe to express my anxiety?

What are my relationship expectations and are they realistic?

Moon in *Libra*

The Moon in Libra seeks to understand itself through its closest bonds and is never *not* wondering what someone else is thinking about them. They seek equilibrium and balance in relationships, often to a fault.

Relationship needs: Conversation

> As an Air sign, the Moon in Libra needs a strong mental connection. While you may be drawn in by physical chemistry, you need to feel a genuine spark on a psychological level for relationship longevity.

Deepen your bond by ... asking your partner to be open to discussion

> Libra Moons often struggle with indecision unless they sense-check their proposed course of action with a trusted sounding-board – usually their partner. That doesn't mean you'll actually follow their advice, but discussing situations is how you process what's going on around you. Explain that in the same way some people need to cry or scream it out, you need to talk it out.

Greatest fear: Rejection

> No Moon fears being disliked as much as a Libran. Even when your phobia is unconscious, you have a tendency to mirror the people around you to put them at ease and gain acceptance.

Constantly compromising to make other people feel comfortable – or like you – means you often hold back from expressing your true needs, opinions and beliefs.

Relationship roadblocks

Dating: Candour

It was probably a Libra Moon who invented ghosting. You'd rather disappear into thin air than have an awkward but frank 'this isn't working out' conversation.

Relationships: Co-dependence

You can be deferential, especially in relationships with dominant personalities. Your desire to keep things balanced means you often bite your tongue to the point of losing your own perspective.

Journal prompts

Am I choosing partners who don't just stimulate me on a physical level, but intellectually too?

Does my partner support my need to workshop my problems?

Do I feel safe to talk about situations freely and honestly as a way of processing emotions?

Do I hide my true feelings for fear of upsetting my partner or initiating confrontation?

Moon in *Scorpio*

The Moon in Scorpio doesn't let its guard down easily, but once they're committed, their attachment is intense. Romantic and intuitive, they crave a deep connection. Physical and emotional sparks are a must-have too; as a Mars-ruled sign, sexual intimacy is the oxygen of their relationships.

Relationship needs: Trust

> Emotionally you may take longer than most to warm up, but give complete and utter buy-in once you've decided to commit. Your own desire to go deep in relationships means you need a partner who isn't afraid to bare their soul and give themselves over completely. Once you open up, your bond and intensity are second to none.

Deepen your bond by ... asking your partner to experiment

> Exploring power and control dynamics in a healthy way can be deeply satisfying. Scorpio energy loves to play on the edge of what's safe. Create a safe container to share your fantasies, then make them come to life.

Greatest fear: Betrayal

> You feel everything on a deep, cellular level – fear included. For a fiercely private, emotionally guarded sign, (finally) letting someone in only to be cast aside is the stuff of nightmares.

Choosing a partner who is both patient and willing to offer plenty of reassurance where it's needed goes a long way to establishing and maintaining a sense of love, trust and security.

Relationship roadblocks

Dating: Control

A Scorpio Moon's sexual magnetism makes casual hook-ups fun, but it's essential you maintain a sense of power in the dynamic. If things develop into a more serious relationship, your reticence to open up can be frustrating – especially if you're with a more upfront sign.

Relationships: Resentment

As a fixed water sign, Scorpio is renowned for holding onto things – both good and bad. Working hard at maintaining an open and honest dialogue in the relationship is important to make sure small emotional wounds don't linger and fester to become major resentments, and in turn much bigger problems.

Journal prompts

Do I feel a complete sense of trust in this relationship?

What do I need to feel safe in relationships?

What actions or words would help me feel more secure and trusting in my relationship?

What helps me feel in control in my relationship?

Moon in *Sagittarius*

Big, bold and full of opinions, Sagittarian Moons have a confidence in love that makes them charismatic and impulsive. Nourished by a sense of adventure and 'what if', they're happiest in relationships that allow them the space to fully express their point of view.

Relationship needs: Flexibility and spontaneity

Variety and freedom fill your cup. That's not to say you need a poly relationship, but you are happiest when there's a degree of flexibility and fun in your romantic dynamic. A partner who's open to trying new things and thrives on spontaneity is important.

Deepen your bond by … asking your partner to make space for you to let off steam

Visceral, fiery and opinionated, you need connection with people who are secure enough to let you get hot and bothered. You want to feel it all – to be consumed by passion, by outrage – then just as quickly, get over it.

Greatest fear: Settling

Sagittarius energy is all about finding meaning and the thrill that comes in their search for a life less ordinary. That doesn't mean life has to be an endless stream of one-night stands, but sharing your life with someone who feels thrilling and is a partner in adventure will truly satisfy you.

Relationship roadblocks

Dating: Commitment

Your tendency to judge can make you a fierce critic and swift deserter. Dating can be a case of 'one and done' if someone doesn't fit in with your world or challenge you in a way that feels exciting and adventurous. Reserving judgement is a skill you need to consciously work at mastering.

Relationships: Compromise

This is not a sign that can sit on the fence or bite its tongue. If you're not on the same page, you'll challenge the other person; not out of spite, but out of passion. You *enjoy* going head-to-head for what you believe in and need someone who can stomach the daily debates.

Journal prompts

Does my relationship feel like an adventure?

Do I feel inspired by my relationship?

Do I feel free to prioritise spontaneity?

Do I feel safe to express my opinions and beliefs?

How can I introduce more spontaneity into my relationships?

Moon in *Capricorn*

Strong, resilient and ambitious, Capricorn Moons are nourished by a sense of commitment and stability in their relationships. They show their love through acts of dedication, reliability and loyalty.

Relationship needs: Understanding and compassion

Naturally guarded, a Capricorn Moon needs a partner who understands your reticence is actually fuelled by fear – not indifference. Your fear of not doing enough/being enough/ giving enough, or simply of being hurt, can come across as aloofness.

Deepen your bond by ... asking your partner to show their commitment through actions

Cap Moons need a relationship with someone who has the patience to chip away at your often-impenetrable emotional armour. A partner who mirrors your proclivity for showing dedication through actions rather than words will make you feel loved and valued.

Greatest fear: Failure

This Saturn-ruled Moon sign is motivated by a need to establish a safe haven – not only for yourself, but the people you love. This makes you susceptible to either working too hard – desperate to climb the mountain and build the castle for your kin – or not letting people in, for fear of letting them down.

Relationship roadblocks

Dating: Guardedness

> You can bet whoever first coined the phrase the 'strong, silent type' dated a Capricorn Moon. You may seem impossible to get to know on a casual basis because you're so guarded. The people who are patient will realise you're worth the wait.

Relationships: Spontaneity

> The steady, resolute nature of the Cap Moon means you're not always free-spirited in love. Responsibility, duty and challenge can almost seem like a turn-on. A laser focus on long-term goals means you can miss incidental opportunities for connection that pop up every day. Set yourself a goal to loosen up and be more playful.

Journal prompts

What two, five and ten year plans do I have for my relationship?

What makes me feel most comfortable expressing my emotions?

What grand gestures or sacrifices have I made to express my love? Does the other person realise/recognise them?

How can I make more space to soften and yield in my relationship?

Moon in *Aquarius*

Analytical and independent, Aquarian Moons are nourished by being with people who share their vision. They are a glorious paradox – needing both space and autonomy, but also craving a strong connection with kindred spirits.

Relationship needs: Shared values

This is not an astro signature that is likely to last in an 'opposites attract' situation. Being with someone who sees the world from a similar framework is essential to long-term satisfaction. Shared values, beliefs and dreams for the future are a non-negotiable.

Deepen your bond by ... asking your partner to be inventive, original and clever

An unconventional gesture of love that also solves a problem will pay dividends when you're trying to impress an Aquarian Moon. If they're stuck on ways to show they care, remind them practical-yet-offbeat signs of affection will make you feel truly loved and understood.

Greatest fear: Being left out

For Aquarian Moons, the emotional drive to belong is almost primal. But that's not the same as going along with the crowd. 'Belonging' is not the same as 'fitting in'. Conformity isn't appealing – in fact, it's often a turn-off for you. But an authentic sense of connection with like-minded people soothes your soul.

Relationship roadblocks

Dating: Detachment

> Your independent approach means you can come across as a bit of an island. On a date, it's easy to misconstrue your self-reliant approach as a kind of cool nonchalance. It's not. If you weren't interested, you genuinely wouldn't waste your time.

Relationships: Autonomy

> Social isolation is your Achilles heel, so it is important you have a partner who understands your need for space to connect with your platonic friends too.

Journal prompts

Does my partner respect, value and share my worldview?

Have I made it clear to my partner my need for solitude is not a sign there's something wrong in the relationship?

What solitary time or extracurricular activities do I need to refill my cup?

What practices or processes help me connect to my emotions, as opposed to simply psychoanalysing them?

Moon in *Pisces*

Gentle, intuitive and deeply compassionate, Pisces Moons are nourished by the act of giving. Their need to love, create and escape means they're romantic and unflinchingly willing to give themselves over wholly to a relationship.

Relationship needs: Intimacy

It sounds silly (don't all relationships need intimacy?) but for Piscean Moons, there's a need to connect with their partner on a deep level. It might be spiritually, it might be creatively, it might be sexually – preferably, it's all of the above. Your choices may not always be conventional or safe, but your desire to experience love as an almost cosmic experience means intimacy is imperative.

Deepen your relationship by … asking your partner to perform grand gestures, just because

There's no way round it, you need Big Time Romance to feel truly satisfied in love. Ask your partner to get creative in how they show they care. Would they write a sonnet? Learn to play your favourite song on guitar? Book a last-minute hotel stay for a Monday night? Any act that's fiercely passionate, spontaneous and creative will deepen your bond.

Greatest fear: Solitude

Piscean Moons are inherently receptive. You are nourished by the act of giving and give yourself wholly and without hesitation. Your desire to give yourself over to a relationship means you can feel almost untethered without one. Your desire for a fairytale romance means without a relationship, you can feel lost – like a vessel overflowing with love, without an outlet.

Relationship roadblocks

Dating: Moving too fast

Your proclivity for being 'in love with love' means you can fall fast and let down your guard quickly or drift from one intense affair to another.

Relationships: Boundaries

A lack of emotional boundaries can be a challenge. The natural receptivity of the Piscean Moon means you can lose yourself in love. Falling for the 'renovators' dream' is a classic Piscean pitfall.

Journal prompts

Do I feel a complete, unwavering, whole-hearted commitment from my partner?

Do I use my relationship to evade responsibility or reality?

What activities help me safely escape into my own little world?

How would I define myself outside my relationship?

What part of my partner am I trying to 'save'?

IV

NOTICE ME

UNDERSTANDING YOUR ASCENDANT

Ever been in a conversation where someone tried to guess your star sign? Chances are they got it wrong, but what you *may* not know is that they possibly came closer than you thought.

While guessing someone's Sun sign isn't always easy, picking their Ascendant is much more straightforward. The reason? The Ascendant – aka the rising sign – represents the energy other people see when they meet us. Often described as 'the mask you wear in the world', in the business of 'You', the Ascendant is your shop front. It's the part of you that people encounter as they walk by.

For most of us, our Ascendant is different to our Sun and Moon signs, which means that our ego (the Sun) and how we *feel* on the inside (the Moon) are not necessarily in sync with how other people perceive us (the Ascendant). To understand your Ascendant is to be armed with a new level of self-awareness and an appreciation of your natural gifts.

When to use this section

Turn to this section when you're trying to make new friends or dive deeper into the dynamics you have in existing relationships – personal, professional or romantic. If you feel you're easily misunderstood – especially on first impression – this is the section for you. It's also useful when you're wanting to make more strategic decisions professionally and want to play to your strengths.

When you want to harness your natural talents

Understanding the qualities of your Ascendant is a bit like finding out you have untapped superpowers. Its qualities come to you easily and naturally; there's no need to force it or work on drawing them out, they're just there, ripe for the taking. Deepening your awareness of your Ascendant can open up pathways of potential you'd previously never considered.

When you want to up your networking game

Having a firm idea of exactly *how* you come across to other people can improve your ability to build relationships. It enables you to choose the environments, careers, communities or pastimes where people are more likely to 'get' you.

Maybe you've been fishing for mates (or dates) in ponds where low-key, earthy types congregate, but it turns out your signature style is far more whimsical.

When you want to understand how people perceive you

With insight into the vibe you're putting out, it's much easier to appreciate why people respond to you the way they do.

For instance, you might feel like a totally submissive teddy bear on the inside (Pisces or Libra Moon perhaps?), but if you have a more intimidating Ascendant – say Capricorn or Aquarius – you're probably fooling everyone into thinking you're a whole lot more no-nonsense than you feel. This knowledge can be especially helpful in work situations where you feel you're reliving the same pattern – like missing out on a promotion – repeatedly. Maybe you feel super-engaged with your job, but your Ascendant reveals you can come across as detached or guarded.

When you want to deepen your astrological awareness

Aside from your Sun and Moon, one of the most important planets in your chart is your chart ruler. Your chart ruler is the planet that rules your Ascendant. It holds an extra special role in your birth chart.

Think of it as your designated driver or cosmic avatar. It sets the tone for how you move through life, where you're going and how you get there. The sign and house where your chart ruler is located adds another layer of nuance to help you deepen your awareness of your natural gifts and predispositions.

How to get the most out of this chapter

Use the info in this chapter to fill out the 'Working with your Ascendant and chart ruler' worksheet available for download at **theastrologyofyou.com** or by scanning the QR code on page 176 to help consolidate all the different qualities of your rising sign (sign, house, element, mode etc.).

Q: What is the
difference between
your Ascendant and
your rising sign?

Technically the term Ascendant refers to the
exact degree of the sign that was rising over the
eastern horizon at the moment you were born
(e.g. nine degrees of Aquarius), while the rising
sign refers to the sign that was rising as a whole
(e.g. Aquarius rising) – but in practice, the two
terms are used interchangeably.

Finding your chart ruler

Ⓐⓢ To figure out your chart ruler, find your Ascendant sign in the table below, then check the corresponding ruling planet. Next, locate that planet in your own chart.

A few signs – Scorpio, Aquarius and Pisces – have different chart rulers depending on whether you follow a modern or traditional approach. Make a note of both, and then check back to the introduction to planets, signs and houses (pages 18–43) to find out about the qualities of your chart ruler. Often one will resonate more than the other, although you may also identify with both in different ways. There's no right or wrong, astrology is personal. Trust your gut.

Here's an example:

My Ascendant is in … Capricorn

The planet that rules Capricorn is … Saturn

In my chart, Saturn is placed … in Libra in the tenth house.

Sign	Traditional ruler	Modern ruler
Aries	Mars	Mars
Taurus	Venus	Venus
Gemini	Mercury	Mercury
Cancer	Moon	Moon
Leo	Sun	Sun
Virgo	Mercury	Mercury
Libra	Venus	Venus
Scorpio	Mars	Pluto
Sagittarius	Jupiter	Jupiter
Capricorn	Saturn	Saturn
Aquarius	Saturn	Uranus
Pisces	Jupiter	Neptune

Understanding your chart ruler

(AS) Your chart ruler carries all kinds of info about your personality and life path. Here are just a few things it represents.

How you approach life

Looking at where your chart ruler is placed adds another level of detail to your chart. The chart ruler represents you in the chart. It describes how you 'do' life. Use the keywords for the signs (pages 20–23), descriptions of the planets (pages 38–41) and themes of the houses (pages 30–34) to help define your signature style.

The flavour of your Ascendant

The placement of your chart ruler adds depth and nuance to your Ascendant sign. This is why you can know someone with Gemini Ascendant who is super-outgoing and playful – maybe they have Mercury in Gemini in the first house – while another is more reserved and low-key – with their chart ruler Mercury placed in Capricorn in the eighth house.

Your interests and affinities

You can think of your chart ruler as the captain of your planetary team. The house and sign location of your chart ruler provides hints as to what areas will be a major focus of your life.

Example

If you are Capricorn Ascendant, then Saturn is the ruler of your chart. If Saturn is placed in Libra in the tenth house, you approach life with serious ambition and an eye on the long game. A tendency to work hard (Saturn) at establishing equality and harmony (Libra) especially at work (tenth house) will be something of a signature approach. With your chart ruler in the tenth house, career and achievement will be a central theme throughout your life.

Your chart ruler through the houses

 The house your chart ruler is placed in adds another layer of context to who you are, what you're drawn to, and where life might take you.

Chart ruler in the first house: The expression of your Ascendant will be clear and present, with a steady focus on the self, independence and physicality which could manifest as a passion for, or life calling in fitness, health, wellbeing or personal style.

Chart ruler in the second house: Money, financial security and self-worth will play a central role in your life. The accumulation – or expenditure – of money and assets may be a core theme.

Chart ruler in the third house: Language, education (especially pre-high school), communication, technology, writing or business may be key themes in your life. You may also have strong ties to siblings or extended family.

Chart ruler in the fourth house: Building a sense of security and contentment behind closed doors will be an important part of your experience. Real estate (think: renovations, property development or interior styling) may also feature strongly on your life path.

Chart ruler in the fifth house: Play, pleasure and fun could be central themes in your life experience. The arts, children or any kind of creative pursuit could also be a priority.

Chart ruler in the sixth house: Showing up for other people – whether personally or professionally – will be a large part of your life story. You might work or volunteer in healthcare, charities or with animals. Your own health and wellbeing could also be a storyline that shapes your experience.

Chart ruler in the seventh house: Being in meaningful relationships – whether that's romantically, professionally, platonically or all of the above – will be of great significance to you. Defining your identity by the partnerships you form will be a core part of your story.

Chart ruler in the eighth house: Sharing your resources and gifts with another person – financial, emotional and physical – will feature strongly in your life story. You might work in a therapeutic setting, or have some calling, interest or experience in realms other people find intimidating or taboo, such as death, sex, trauma or finance.

Chart ruler in the ninth house: A strong calling to see the world or expand your worldview through travel, religion or immersion in other cultures will shape your experience. You may be drawn to a life path connected to law, media, academia or the esoteric, or live overseas.

Chart ruler in the tenth house: Professional accomplishment and public reputation will be a strong focus in your life story. You could be someone who dreams of a big career, professional accolades or even fame. Your life path is punctuated by a need to be seen and achieve your goals in a public forum.

Chart ruler in the eleventh house: A sense of connection to friends, community or chosen family will be an essential part of your path. You may be drawn to environments or relationships where you feel like you're part of some bigger movement or cause.

Chart ruler in the twelfth house: Your expression of your Ascendant will be more understated and less obvious. You might crave periods of solitude or be drawn to deep spiritual practices. Your life path may take you to isolated places – geographically, socially, psychologically or spiritually.

Planets in aspect to the Ascendant

Planets in aspect to the Ascendant degree (square or opposition) bring an electrifying element to the Ascendant's qualities. The planet making a hard aspect can feel unwieldy or at odds with the Ascendant, like an interfering noise scrambling its signal, but can also offer an activating energy that supercharges its qualities.

Planets conjunct the Ascendant degree are central to the way you move through the world. For instance, people with Venus on the Ascendant are often magnetic and charismatic, while people with Jupiter on the Ascendant tend to have boundless confidence.

Planets in supporting aspects (trines or sextiles) to the Ascendant degree are like natural gifts that can help bolster your Ascendant qualities and add extra charm or flair to how you express your Ascendant. They are less noticeable than other aspects and shine brightest when you consciously choose to capitalise on them – especially trines.

Aries Ascendant

Your chart ruler: Mars

How other people see you: With your Ascendant in Aries, taking up space and initiating action are natural talents. Even if you don't *feel* especially confident on the inside, there's a fiery determination about your natural energy that makes people sit up and take notice.

How to tap into your natural gifts: Making things happen is the magic of Mars-ruled Aries. Initiation, spark and leadership help get the fire started. Trust yourself to get involved when other signs are still second-guessing what to do next.

Pressure points: The Aries Ascendant can at times come across as a little forceful or single-minded (in varying degrees, depending on where your Mars is placed). Your innate self-assurance can cause others to back down and let you take charge. If you find yourself exhausted from leading (or fighting), considering stepping back and letting other people take the reins for a change.

Taurus Ascendant

Your chart ruler: Venus

How other people see you: With your Ascendant in Taurus, you move through the world with a palpable appreciation for beauty. You may be an avid collector, a creative or exude a sense of tranquillity and calm. Even if your mind is frenetic, on the surface you seem as though you know where you're headed.

How to tap into your natural gifts: A natural affinity for beautiful things – whether it's making the perfect cacio e pepe, styling a vignette or singing with perfect pitch – makes you fun to be around. Showcase your goddess-given talents by taking the lead in situations that could benefit from a touch of beauty.

Pressure points: The Taurus Ascendant can appear wedded to routine and, worst-case scenario, inflexible. Be mindful that your low-key confidence can come across as resistant to change and unreceptive to feedback – even if you don't feel you're either of those things on the inside.

Gemini Ascendant

Your chart ruler: Mercury

How other people see you: An innate multiplicity means there's something about you that's hard to define. Maybe you're into meditation ... but you're also passionate about football. There's a beauty in your oddity that draws people in and keeps them guessing.

How to tap into your natural gifts: You are multitudes, and *that* is your superpower! A chameleon-like quality means people find you inimitable – lean into it! Your breadth of interests means you can talk to almost anyone, but also makes you hard to pre-empt. Own it! There's a lot to be said for not being an open book.

Pressure points: There are two kinds of people in this world: those who will find your eclectic tastes charming, and those who will find it confusing. People like putting other people in boxes and often a Gemini Ascendant just won't fit the mould. That's OK. You can't please everyone all the time.

Cancer Ascendant

Your chart ruler: The Moon

How other people see you: With a Cancer Ascendant, your signature blend of caring-yet-competent means you're a magnet for people looking for support. With the Moon as your chart ruler, there's a natural receptivity that means folks just can't help but unload on you, even when you didn't ask them to share their feelings or problems.

How to tap into your natural gifts: A natural sensitivity to your environment makes you highly attuned to what's going on around you. Your emotional intelligence makes you an excellent ally in times of stress or hardship. Play to your strengths by looking for opportunities that value intuition and empathy.

Pressure points: A tendency to keep your guard up, especially around new people, can make you seem a tad stand-offish. Know that while you may feel like you're being outrageously outgoing from the outside, you're probably keeping a reasonably low profile.

Leo Ascendant

Your chart ruler: The Sun

How other people see you: There's a brightness and optimism with a Leo Ascendant that draws other people in. Exactly how extroverted you are depends on what house and sign your Sun (your chart ruler) is placed. Some will be more outgoing than others, but all will have a generosity of spirit that people gravitate towards.

How to tap into your natural gifts: One of the most overlooked gifts of Leo energy is its reliability. As a fixed sign, there's a steadiness and fortitude to the way you move through the world that makes you a dependable ally. Surprise people by showing your conviction matches that famous Leo courage.

Pressure points: Like any Leo placement, pride can become a source of tension in your relationships. Be mindful that you may come across as impenetrably poised. A lack of vulnerability can be intimidating to other people or maybe even seem a little insensitive. Making an effort to show your emotions helps you seem a little less unapproachable.

Virgo Ascendant

Your chart ruler: Mercury

How other people see you: Did somebody say 'capable'? Your mind-over-matter pragmatism makes you a magnet for the less organised among us (which is basically everyone). Untangling other people's knotty cords – emotionally, physically and materially, is a role you slip into easily, often to your own detriment.

How to tap into your natural gifts: Flexible, observant and considered, you're a natural-born fixer who finds it hard not to step in and help out – even when your own plate is overflowing. Look for opportunities where you will be acknowledged (and remunerated!) for your can-do attitude.

Pressure points: Boundaries are a life-long lesson. You are capable of enforcing parameters although it may not be easy (depending on where Mercury, your chart ruler, is placed). Apply that famous Virgo sense of discernment and say 'no' more often to avoid overcommitting and burning yourself out.

Libra Ascendant

Your chart ruler: Venus

How other people see you: A natural ability to adjust your façade means you can meet just about anyone on their level in a warm, genuine way, and make them feel like they're the only person in the room. 'Charm offensive' is your default mode.

How to tap into your natural gifts: Believe it or not, social anxiety is a real thing that most people suffer from, at some point in their lives. Your genuine ease for being around people and facilitating connections is an asset. Look for opportunities where you can bring people together and create a sense of social harmony.

Pressure points: With an ability to 'change your spots' to make those around you feel more comfortable, it's not uncommon to have your sincerity questioned. Understanding that some people – usually those less socially gifted – may find your charms threatening, can help you make sense of unexplained hostility.

Scorpio Ascendant

Your chart ruler: Mars, Pluto

How other people see you: Not all Scorpios look like Wednesday Addams. There's a lot more going on beneath the surface than meets the eye. What you see is not necessarily what you get. Sure, you can turn it on when you need to, but what others may not realise is that you're actually quite a closed book. This makes you a mysterious muse and a potentially formidable foe.

How to tap into your natural gifts: There's a lot to be said for having a great poker face. Gravitating towards environments that value keen powers of perception teamed with a cool façade (think: medical settings, therapeutic scenarios and client-facing work) will give you the opportunity to play to your natural strengths.

Pressure points: Getting past your deceptively impermeable exterior is easier said than done. Boundaries are great, but not everyone has an ulterior motive. Trust your instincts when someone seems a bit dodgy, but don't build walls so high that no one can get in.

Sagittarius Ascendant

Your chart ruler: Jupiter

How other people see you: To the outside world, you are confident in your opinions and possibly a wee bit cavalier in your approach, even if you feel completely differently on the inside. A perceived optimism and willingness to take a chance means opportunities often come a-knockin' – even when you aren't looking for them.

How to tap into your natural gifts: A fear of the unknown is a major threat for most people, but chances are you're prepared to try your luck – even when the odds are 50/50. Seeking out environments and relationships where a playful 'let's give it a go' mindset is championed will be a great fit for your natural capabilities.

Pressure points: That seemingly boundless well of confidence can come across as a little overpowering, especially to more shy, retiring types. Stepping back and encouraging those who aren't quite as forthcoming as you to share their perspective will go a long way towards improving diplomatic relations and showing your sensitivity.

Capricorn Ascendant

Your chart ruler: Saturn

How other people see you: When all else fails, people turn to a Capricorn Ascendant to pick up the slack and finish the job. Your sense of calm amid chaos can be both inspiring and a little bit intimidating to those around you.

How to tap into your natural gifts: Resilience and resolve run deep in your veins. As unglamorous as it may sound, the long way is often the most fulfilling and almost always the least crowded. Play to your persistence and appetite for hard work by choosing the more challenging but ultimately more rewarding path; it's almost always your safest and most satisfying bet.

Pressure points: Depending on where your Saturn (your chart ruler) is placed you'll fall somewhere on the 'steely determination' spectrum. Just because you're not super-flashy doesn't mean people won't notice how capable you are. Always being left to clean up other people's mess is an occupational hazard for Capricorn Ascendants. Flex those famous Capricorn boundaries to make sure you're not left steering a sinking ship.

Aquarius Ascendant

Your chart ruler: Saturn, Uranus

How other people see you: Analytical, innovative and a little bit quirky, there's something out of the ordinary about an Aquarian Ascendant. As a fixed Air sign, you're both composed and resolute in the way you move through the world, which comes across as cool, calm and usually a tad stand-offish.

How to tap into your natural gifts: There is an undeniably thoughtful side to this Aquarius placement that means you can't help but take life a little bit seriously. Your ability to think outside the box and stay focused on a solution – especially when everyone around you is getting caught up in how they feel – makes you an invaluable problem-solver. Find places, relationships and roles where you can let that analytical light shine.

Pressure points: 'Emotionally detached' is a description that gets levelled at Aquarian Ascendants pretty regularly – and for good reason. Your tendency to rationalise situations and behaviour means you're often lost in thought and not overly identified with emotional territory. It doesn't mean you don't care – but that 1000-yard gaze can suggest otherwise.

Pisces Ascendant

Your chart ruler: Jupiter, Neptune

How other people see you: Creative, intuitive and perceptive, there's an other-worldly quality to Pisces rising people. If the rest of your chart is especially gritty or fiery (think: big Earth or Fire energy) other people may underestimate you.

How to tap into your natural gifts: Your expansive approach to life means you're gifted at seeing the deeper wisdom in situations – even when they're less than ideal. Exploring opportunities and relationships that encourage you to zoom out and consider the bigger picture will harness your visionary approach and help you play to your strengths.

Pressure points: The Piscean tendency to energetically absorb what's going on around you means you're highly sensitive to your environment – for better or worse. Getting swept away in other people's stuff – emotional baggage, value systems or day-to-day plans – is a real danger. Keeping firm boundaries isn't easy, but it is crucial for your wellbeing. Likewise persisting with toxic situations/environments/relationships will knock you around much more than other signs. Refining your energetic hygiene will be an ongoing challenge.

V

TEACH ME

AS

ME

UNDERSTANDING YOUR NODES

In evolutionary astrology, the Moon's Nodes represent where you've come from and what you've come to learn on a soul level. You can use them to frame your life experience, identify recurrent patterns and help you illuminate a path to a new way of being.

What is evolutionary astrology?

Evolutionary astrology uses specialised interpretive techniques of the Moon's Nodes to discover a soul's karmic path.

A belief in reincarnation and a conviction that the birth chart holds pivotal information about a soul's evolutionary intention are central to this approach.

Steven Forrest pioneered the practice in his iconic book *Yesterday's Sky: Astrology and Reincarnation* – a must-read for anyone intrigued by this fascinating corner of the astrological world. If you're interested in going deeper, Steven teaches at the Forrest Center for Evolutionary Astrology **www.forrestastrology.center** or visit **forrestastrology.com**.

How to get the most out of this chapter

First, use the info in this chapter to fill out the 'Working with your North and South Nodes' worksheet available at **theastrologyofyou.com** or by scanning the QR code on page 176 to consolidate all the different qualities of your Nodes (sign, house, element, mode, etc.). Next, use the journal prompts at the end of your nodal profile as a way to explore what your soul has come here to resolve, heal and learn.

What exactly are the Nodes?

☊ ☋ The Nodes are intersecting points in space between the ecliptic (the plane of the Earth's orbit around the Sun) and the Moon's orbit around the Earth. They are points in space, not actual planets or luminaries.

The South Node is where the Moon crosses the path of the ecliptic, heading south, and in evolutionary astrology it represents the past. The North Node is where the Moon crosses the path of the ecliptic as it heads north, representing future potential.

The Nodes change signs about every eighteen months, meaning people born around the same time share the same nodal signature. That's not to say everyone born within that time frame shares the exact same soul purpose – the detail comes from where the Nodes are placed in your chart, as well as the location of their planetary rulers. As a starting point, delving into the sign and house of your North and South Nodes will help you understand your karmic baggage and soul purpose.

All about the South Node

☋ The South Node is familiar

Whichever way you approach it, the South Node is familiar territory. If you're open to the idea of reincarnation, you can think of it as a way of moving through the world that you've been practising for lifetimes. It is karmic baggage you've lugged into this life.

If you don't believe in reincarnation, you can think of it as an inherent energy you were born with. Another way to approach the South Node is as ancestral energy – a karmic tie to your family lineage. It's quite common to see similarities between the attributes of your South Node and the lived experience of your parents or grandparents.

☋ The South Node is limiting

When we look at the South Node in a sign, we draw on its less attractive traits since it's the less appealing qualities that manifest as emotional baggage. It describes qualities and behavioural patterns that are second nature and points to problems or issues that need to be worked through and resolved in this lifetime.

☋ The South Node is comfortable

When we are stuck, scared, stressed or overwhelmed, the South Node is the energy we embody without thinking. It is the knee-jerk reaction we automatically default to – like the compulsion to bite your nails when you're anxious. When you've had a bad day, slipping into the South Node feels good because it's familiar. Like a pair of old sweatpants you just can't bring yourself to throw out, it's what you pull on to get comfortable.

All about the North Node

☊   **The North Node is the opposite of the South Node**

The North Node, on the other hand, is quite literally the other end of the spectrum. It represents the energy your soul was born to explore in this lifetime. From a technical perspective, it is always the sign exactly opposite the South Node in the wheel of the zodiac. This means it will be at odds with your South Node, but also exists on a common axis.

☊   **The North Node is unfamiliar**

The qualities of the North Node are usually uncomfortable or even alien. 'Foreign' is a word that comes up a lot in readings when I start to describe the energy of the North Node. It describes a way of moving through the world or approaching problems that feels completely new. It's your least obvious course of action. Imagine it as an item of clothing you've never even considered wearing, let alone embracing on a daily basis.

☊   **The North Node is challenging**

Often, when people first hear about the qualities of their North Node, they cringe or shudder at the thought of embodying that energy. This is almost always an indication that you're getting to a place of vulnerability and growth. Whenever you have a visceral reaction, it's like a flashing light that THIS is where the work is to be done.

☊ The North Node is exhilarating

Embodying the qualities of the North Node rarely comes naturally. Like learning a new skill, the North Node almost always takes effort and time. Of course, there's nothing in your chart that says you must walk the North Node path. Many people are happily stuck in their South Node their entire life. How much you choose to accept the challenges of the North Node is up to you. But if you do choose to follow your North Node, once you get past the initial discomfort, you often find a tremendous sense of satisfaction and think, 'I can't believe I didn't try this sooner!'

When to use this section

The Nodes carry perhaps the broadest brushstrokes of any energy explored in this book. They offer a big-picture perspective you can use on any decision – whether it's life-changing or insignificant. I always encourage clients to ask, 'What would my North Node do?'

When you're feeling completely lost

Perhaps one of their most powerful uses is for rerouting your soul's GPS. The Nodes offer a deeply healing framework when you're feeling lost. They can help steer you somewhere new and exciting when you're seeking direction, and illuminate a path (almost always entirely outside your comfort zone) that promises new adventures, experiences and, most of all, big soul growth.

When you find yourself staring at a 'WRONG WAY, GO BACK' sign (figuratively speaking), the Nodes can help you work out the next best step. They are the ultimate jumping-off point for 'Where to from here?' questions. Reflecting on the South Node and the North Node responses to a situation helps you clarify what your options are – and which way might serve you best.

When you're wondering what's missing

When everything looks OK on paper, but you still feel like something is missing, the Nodes are the perfect place to dig deep. Turn to the Nodes when life is ticking along, but you're still feeling unfulfilled. Chances are, that something extra you're searching for is a sprinkling of North Node magic.

When you're desperate to make a change

The Nodes are a great place to look when you find yourself dealing with the same problems again and again. Take a look at your Nodes and you'll see the recurrent patterns we default to when we're living life on autopilot or from a place of fear. The Nodes identify the unconscious decision-making process you switch to, especially when you're feeling freaked out. Reflecting on what the South and North Node responses are (or might have been if you're thinking about past mistakes) helps identify your options, and figure out which way might yield very different results.

How to embrace your Nodes

Find a North Node muse

Because the energy of the North Node is almost always foreign, it can be hard to understand how to embody those qualities in everyday life. One fun exercise to try is to research someone who carries a strong signature of that sign. It could be a friend or family member, or even someone in the public eye who has their Sun, Moon or rising in that sign. Reflect on how they embody the qualities of that sign, and experiment with using them as a muse. How do they approach life? How do they approach tough decisions? What do they prioritise? What can you learn from their way of doing things?

Look for common ground

Although they are always opposing signs, there is a common ground between the North and South Nodes. Their energetic axis shows how they approach a similar issue from opposite ends of the spectrum.

For example, Virgo is at the opposite side of the zodiac to Pisces. Their approach and perspective to life are completely different, and yet both signs at their core are concerned with healing. Both are motivated by compassion, empathy and a desire to be of service – one earthy and practical (Virgo), the other big-picture and deeply spiritual (Pisces). Recognising the bridge between your South and North Nodes helps you identify a central theme to your soul's path. Embracing the bridge helps you integrate and honour your karmic past while embodying your nodal potential.

The Nodes through the houses

☋ ☊ For a deeper understanding of your nodal energy, consider the house where your Nodes are located. For more about the houses turn to pages 28–35.

South Node in the first house, North Node in the seventh house reflects a karmic pattern of being excessively self-willed, perhaps even a lone wolf, or having an unhealthy preoccupation on the self. This could manifest as a fixation with body image, appearance or how you're perceived by other people. Your path in this lifetime is to embrace the joy of collaboration. One-on-one partnerships in work, and in life, will be a source of fulfilment if you choose to love and share with a co-pilot.

South Node in the second house, North Node in the eighth house reflects a karmic pattern around financial or material issues. There could be a fear around never having enough, a preoccupation with status symbols, or a wariness of getting financially involved with other people. Your path in this lifetime is learning to trust and share your resources in a healthy way – emotionally, physically and financially – this will be a source of enlightenment. Resisting the urge to numb out by acquiring more 'stuff' and delving into the deeper issues fuelling your material cravings will be healing.

South Node in the third house, North Node in the ninth house reflects a karmic pattern of playing small when you're faced with a threat. You might take on the role of the student, or keep yourself busy with logistics and admin in an effort to avoid addressing bigger, more philosophical issues. Your path in this lifetime is to shake off the rookie mentality and become more of an authority. Answering the call to expand your horizons, get out of your comfort zone and experience the world as a little fish in a big pond. Travel – especially overseas – higher learning and spiritual practices could be truly rewarding.

South Node in the fourth house, North Node in the tenth house
reflects a karmic pattern of putting family expectations ahead of your own personal ambitions. You might use familial responsibilities as an excuse for not exploring your own goals, or hide behind the drudgery of household pressures to avoid taking a chance on a career that's always called your name. Your path in this lifetime is to chase the big dreams that keep you awake at night, and balance your home and family life with your own personal goals.

South Node in the fifth house, North Node in the eleventh house
reflects a karmic pattern where a lack of boundaries and a tendency towards excess defined your previous experiences. Avoiding reality – whether it's with food, drugs, sex, or shopping – could be a real temptation. Whatever your poison, having a little too much of a good time may block your chance of finding meaning and connection. Your path this lifetime is to embrace experiences where you can feel a part of something bigger and shift the focus away from instant gratification. Community involvement, social justice or advocating on behalf of a group could all be hugely rewarding pathways.

South Node in the sixth house, North Node in the twelfth house
reflects a karmic path of burying yourself in responsibility. Whether it's being a slave to your job, your kids or your partner, there's a sense of martyrdom where you run yourself ragged. In times of stress, taking on *more* responsibility is often a coping mechanism to help you numb out and avoid addressing your own needs. Your path in this lifetime is to embrace solitude. To relinquish control and learn how to enjoy the freedom of having blank space in your calendar. Experiment with how it feels to do less, prioritise introspection, and say 'no' to energetic vampires.

South Node in the seventh house, North Node in the first house
reflects a karmic path of someone who can be overly deferential in the face of uncertainty. You may be prone to co-dependency, struggle with decision-making and/or dread trying things on your own. Your path in this lifetime is to develop a sense of independence and trust your gut. Making decisions in your best interest, first and foremost.

Learning to put your needs ahead of other people's, especially a partner, will be a lifelong lesson.

South Node in the eighth house, North Node in the second house reflects a karmic path rooted in a lack of agency. Whether it's financial, energetic, physical, or all of the above, feeling or behaving from a position of powerlessness could be a familiar path. Your challenge in this lifetime is to develop a sense of personal power. Doing things to help you establish a sense of independent security and self-worth, outside of anyone else's expectations, is key. Building your own financial independence and doing life on your own terms will support your growth.

South Node in the ninth house, North Node in the third house reflects a karmic pattern of getting caught up in big ideas, high-falutin paths or even religion at the expense of your everyday commitments. It may manifest as a tendency to avoid or reject mundane responsibilities or an aversion to putting down roots. You may be prone to assuming the role of teacher – even when you aren't qualified. Your path in this lifetime is to celebrate all that you *don't* know, to acknowledge your blind spots and embrace the experience of being a student rather than trying to assume the role of guru. Finding wisdom and wonder in your own backyard/neighbourhood could prove deeply rewarding.

South Node in the tenth house, North Node in the fourth house reflects a karmic path of being preoccupied with achievement and success, especially when it comes to career and reputation. It could manifest as workaholic tendencies or a pattern of using your work as an excuse to avoid intimacy, especially at home. Your path in this lifetime is to create a safe, nourishing environment – emotionally and physically – behind closed doors. To prioritise family, or chosen family, and establish boundaries with your work.

South Node in the eleventh house, North Node in the fifth house reflects a karmic past rooted in groupthink. It can manifest as a tendency to follow the crowd, to worry unnecessarily about how you (or your ideas/work/actions) will be received by your peers or a pattern of prioritising ideology or a macro cause ahead of your own needs. Your path in this lifetime is to lighten up, to learn how to have more fun, to make space for joy, pleasure and creativity and, most of all, to embrace your individuality.

South Node in the twelfth house, North Node in the sixth house reflects a karmic path where isolation, withdrawal and avoidance are recurrent patterns. It can manifest in this lifetime as a tendency to check out from everyday life (either physically escape, or with substances), and/or shut down in the face of stress. You may assume you have to face things alone and emotionally withdraw in times of hardship. Your path in this lifetime is to find a sense of stability and groundedness in routine; to embrace responsibility, to find joy through the act of caring for others, and find solace in service.

Planets in aspect to the Nodes

☋ ☊ Whether you approach the Nodes as the key to understanding your past life story or prefer the approach of reading them as an ancestral legacy, interpreting the aspects they make to other planets adds more detail to your story.

Planets conjunct the South Node (opposing the North Node)

A planet conjunct the South Node imbues it with its qualities, adding another note to its flavour – like adding another stand-out ingredient (the planet) to a sauce (the South Node); think anchovies to Napoletana.

From a past life perspective it offers more detail on who you were and the challenges you faced. For example, Mars conjunct the South Node would give a very Mars-y flavour to your past life story, where anger, aggression and domination were key themes in your life.

From an ancestral lineage perspective it adds detail to the karmic baggage passed down the generations. Whether you read it as a past life or an ancestral energy, it details how the energy manifests in the present.

Because it is always opposing the North Node, it represents another roadblock you'll encounter trying to embody the qualities of the North Node in this lifetime.

Planets conjunct the North Node (opposing the South Node)

Similarly, a planet conjunct the North Node adds more information about the path you were born to explore.

As it always opposes the South Node, it can represent a block. From a past life perspective it might have been a situation where you came off second-best or a person who obstructed you from reaching your potential.

Ancestrally, it can represent a situation that thwarted previous generations. The planet may point to a common archetype in the family. For example, the Sun in Scorpio as the controlling, divisive patriarch.

Planets squaring the North and South Node

Like planets making an opposition to the Nodes, planets squaring the Nodes offer further information on the difficulties you – or your family – faced, and what you need to overcome in this lifetime.

In the context of past lives, they represent unresolved issues. The planet's qualities describe loose ends requiring some action to resolve them once and for all.

From an ancestral point of view, the planet can describe an ongoing hang-up or problem that has been handed down generations – for example, Venus in Virgo squaring the Nodes might represent a struggle to find joy outside of work.

Drawing on the planet's more positive qualities can offer some assistance in moving beyond the block in this life, and propel you on the North Node path. For instance, playing to Venus in Virgo's delight in detail, you might find a creative outlet and an escape from work by experimenting with stop-motion animation.

Planets making soft aspects to the Nodes

Planets making soft aspects to the South Node represent a personal quality, situation or person who may have been supportive in your past life although ultimately, they weren't enough to help you move beyond the bigger setbacks.

In the context of ancestors, they could represent a supportive archetype within your family – the Moon in Cancer could represent a selfless and compassionate mother figure.

By their nature, the planets will also make soft aspects to the North Node (planets trine the South Node will sextile the North Node and vice versa), and may offer some useful energetic back-up to follow the North Node path in this lifetime.

The North Node in *Aries* and the South Node in *Libra*

Energetic axis the self vs. others

Keywords leadership, courage, decisiveness

Major life lessons

- ◯   Mastering the art of healthy assertiveness
- ◯   Learning to lead without apology
- ◯   Making decisions without consulting others

Where you've come from the Libra South Node

With a Libra South Node, keeping the peace and playing nice are a natural reflex. This South Node has a tendency to seek validation from others and may suffer from indecision, anxiety and analysis paralysis. Underneath a calm façade, you still get frustrated or annoyed with people – you're only human – but expressing anger or asserting yourself can be difficult. Remember, avoiding conflict only internalises your emotions.

What you've come here to learn the Aries North Node

An Aries North Node is a karmic invitation to learn the art of healthy assertion. Your mission is to figure out what you like and what you don't, without getting caught up in other people's opinions, and finding the courage to ask for what you want.

This lifetime is about learning to stand up for yourself and getting comfortable with rocking the boat. Learning how to make decisions quickly and trust yourself. Aries energy isn't afraid to take action;

when it makes mistakes, it doesn't waste energy worrying about it, the past is the past. This North Node wants you to toughen up and get on with it.

Mindful mantras

- ◯ Anger is a valid and necessary emotion

- ◯ Taking up space is not a crime

- ◯ I hold all the answers within me

- ◯ Not everyone I meet will like me, and that's OK

- ◯ Being honest is as admirable as being nice

Journal prompts

What was my family's reaction towards me expressing anger when I was growing up?

When do I notice anger well up, but refrain from expressing it? What needs are not being met at that moment?

When do I defer to others for guidance?

When am I most likely to seek approval from other people?

When do I refrain from expressing my opinions or emotions for fear of upsetting the status quo?

What do I believe might happen if I expressed my emotions and/or opinions honestly as they arise in the moment?

The North Node in *Taurus* and the South Node in *Scorpio*

Energetic axis safety vs. suspicion

Keywords security, pleasure, trust

Major life lessons

- ○ Learning to trust with an open heart

- ○ Building a sense of material and emotional stability

- ○ Relinquishing the need for control in relationships

Where you've come from the Scorpio South Node

The South Node in Scorpio reflects a karmic story where control, power and intense situations shaped your experiences. You may have lived life where you felt under threat, or found yourself in scenarios that felt unsafe.

In this lifetime, opening up and trusting people can be difficult. You may be overly guarded, with an expectation that people or situations are not as they appear. Another manifestation is an attraction to relationships with destructive power dynamics. A tendency to fixate on issues/interests/people in an obsessive way is also a possible pitfall of this placement.

What you've come here to learn the Taurus North Node

The North Node in Taurus is an invitation to explore and embrace pleasure, for pleasure's sake. It's quite simply a karmic reminder to lighten up. Your work is to build a life of safety, comfort and creative fulfilment. Prioritising the things that make you *feel* good on a visceral level and seeking out relationships that make you feel safe, loved and secure – both physically and emotionally – are key. Prioritising time in nature is important, as is finding a creative outlet that lights you up. Coming back to your body, trusting yourself, experimenting with the notion that maybe things will work out. Creating a safe place, where there is calm, beauty, and above all else where you feel secure enough to let your guard down and relax is essential.

Mindful mantras

- ○ I live life with a sense of ease and flow
- ○ I am safe, protected and loved
- ○ Pain is not an inevitable by-product of love
- ○ I am in complete control of my body, mind and emotions
- ○ Abundance flows easily to me
- ○ My body is a sacred gift for creativity and pleasure

Journal prompts

What course of action would make me feel most secure – emotionally, physically and financially?

What activities help me reconnect to my body and connect with a deeper sense of pleasure?

When have I trusted someone and things have turned out OK?

What types of encounters and activities in nature help me feel grounded and at ease?

What creative pursuits help me switch off and feel truly in the moment?

The North Node in *Gemini* and the South Node in *Sagittarius*

Energetic axis fluidity vs. dogma

Keywords experimentation, play, flexibility

Major life lessons

- Relinquishing the need to have the final word

- Letting go of labels

- Getting comfortable with ambiguity

- Giving yourself permission to play and experiment

- Allowing other people – and yourself – to make mistakes

Where you've come from the Sagittarius South Node

The South Node in Sagittarius speaks to a karmic past deeply rooted in ideology. You likely embodied 'my way or the highway' energy, unwaveringly rigid in your point of view. You may have been inherently restless or had an inability to settle in one place for too long.

In this lifetime, your South Node can flare up as a big know-it-all energy. A self-righteous streak fuels a need to have the final say, and dismiss anyone who doesn't agree with you. A Sagittarian South Node can also resist commitment or move around endlessly in search of somewhere (or someone) truly meaningful.

What you've come here to learn the Gemini North Node

The North Node in Gemini is an invitation to broaden your perspective. It is about letting go of a binary approach to life and allowing yourself to experience *all* the things. You don't have to choose between being an accountant OR a reiki master; you can be both! When you're making decisions, exploring what it feels like to replace 'or' with 'and' is key. Being fluid – whether it's your job, your sexuality, your spiritual beliefs or all of the above – is big Gemini North Node energy. You don't have to choose, you can do it all, try it all. Getting comfortable with trial and error is essential. Embracing the joy of two-way conversation rather than just talking 'at' people. Finding the lightness, curiosity and the learning in situations – even when they feel heavy – is Gemini North Node to a tee.

Mindful mantras

- ◯ Mistakes are a learning opportunity

- ◯ I am a glorious multitude of contradictions

- ◯ I don't have all the answers ... and that is OK

- ◯ Experimentation is the life source of my creative flow

- ◯ Selflessly listening yields the most profound insights

Journal prompts

What have I learnt from my biggest mistakes?

How often do I listen to simply listen, rather than listen, waiting to respond?

What activities or interests have I always been curious to learn more about?

What relationships, situations or environments make me feel most playful?

What happens when I replace 'either' with 'and'?

The North Node in *Cancer* and the South Node in *Capricorn*

Energetic axis compassion vs. grit

Keywords receptivity, empathy, sensitivity

Major life lessons

○ Relaxing your attachment to achievement

○ Dropping the expectation you must fend for yourself

○ Finding fulfilment in family – chosen or biological

○ Learning to trust your intuition rather than rely on rules

Where you've come from the Capricorn South Node

The South Node in Capricorn reflects energetic baggage rooted in responsibility, ambition and gravitas. An unflinching determination to achieve at all costs defined your karmic past. Your approach was serious, relentless and unemotional – with an expectation that life will be difficult and lonely. A fear of poverty might have been a motivating factor.

In this lifetime, it can manifest as an unhealthy attachment to work. You might feel overly invested in reaching milestones of success, fuelled by a scarcity mentality. A reluctance to express vulnerability, and a sense of realism veering on pessimism can also be an issue.

What you've come here to learn the Cancer North Node

The North Node in Cancer is an invitation to soften and allow life to happen. Acknowledging your sensitivity, and finding power in vulnerability, is a major life lesson. Learning how to feel your feelings – and actually share them – is important. Practising how to sit with difficult emotions when they arise rather than pushing them aside and 'getting on with things' is key. This placement is about finding fulfilment, caring for someone else and exploring what family means to you. This by no means has to be a traditional set-up, but finding your people and sticking together will bring immeasurable joy. Nurturing someone – or something – else will yield life's greatest gifts.

Mindful mantras

- Vulnerability is not a sign of weakness

- I trust what's coming is meant for me

- My material success is not a measure of my worth

- Strength and softness are not mutually exclusive

- Tears are a constructive way to process emotions

Journal prompts

When was the last time I quit pushing and just let things happen?

How can I allow myself more space to let big feelings move through me?

What relationships make me feel safe to open up and express my vulnerability?

When have I prioritised connection over achievement?

The North Node in *Leo*
and the South Node in *Aquarius*

Energetic axis the individual vs. the group

Keywords pride, confidence, visibility

Major life lessons

- ○ Getting comfortable with being in the spotlight

- ○ Resisting the urge to go along with the crowd

- ○ Leaning into your creativity rather than overthinking things

- ○ Shining your light and being received by other people

Where you've come from the Aquarius South Node

With an Aquarius South Node, your karmic baggage is around letting your individual needs take a backseat in favour of the greater good. You may have been part of a political, religious group or subculture that, while tight-knit, had a distinct outsider quality to it. Rationalising your loss of personal agency would have been a strong signature, as well as rejecting any personal creative callings.

In this lifetime, the South Node can show up as a tendency to go along with the crowd. It most commonly presents as a fear of being seen or standing out. You may default to a 'power in numbers' position, where you don't allow yourself to express (or even explore) your own feelings about issues or feel unwilling to put yourself out there – especially creatively.

What you've come here to learn the Leo North Node

A Leo North Node is a karmic invitation to let your light shine! Your mission is to get more comfortable with being seen. Stepping into the spotlight, raising your voice and sharing your creative gifts with the world are key. Resisting the temptation to hang back with the pack and go along with what everyone else is doing will be a challenge worth pursuing. Honouring the fact that you are an inherently creative being, and letting yourself explore that in a way that feels exciting and energising is essential. Doing things that feel a little bit scary and a whole lot of fun (as opposed to noble, selfless or worthy) is a great starting point.

Mindful mantras

- It's OK for me to be seen

- I am proud of all that I have achieved

- I have the courage to take on new challenges alone

- It is safe for me to take up space and shine my light

- My individual needs are valid considerations when I am making decisions

---

Journal prompts

When do I let myself be swept away with the group?

How do I feel in my heart?

When (and with whom) do I feel safe to be seen?

What creative outlet have I always dreamt of exploring?

When (and with whom) do I feel most courageous?

The North Node in *Virgo* and the South Node in *Pisces*

Energetic axis refinement vs. fluidity

Keywords selectiveness, groundedness, order

Major life lessons

- ◯ Becoming selective with your compassion
- ◯ Finding stability through order and process
- ◯ Learning to love problem-solving
- ◯ Developing routines that support your wellbeing

Where you've come from the Pisces South Node

A South Node in Pisces reflects karmic baggage around boundaries. There's a soul history of needing to save people around you, or of throwing yourself into projects or relationships without consideration for the practical consequences.

In this lifetime, it can feel innately untethered. Escapism, fantasy and a lack of discernment can lead to destructive outcomes. You may have the urge to check out from reality or bury your head in the sand. You may fall in love often and quickly. It can also manifest as a kind of reckless compassion where you give so much of yourself, you lose your own sense of identity and suffer from emotional burnout.

What you've come here to learn the Virgo North Node

A Virgo North Node is a karmic invitation to become more discerning with how and where you focus your energy. Your compassionate heart is a superpower you should guard wisely – not everyone is entitled to have a turn. One of your greatest challenges will be to learn how to say 'no' without being overwhelmed by guilt. The art of respectful, loving boundaries is a core skill to be mastered. Stability is also important. Learning to come back to your body, establishing more earthy practices where you can keep at least one foot in reality, will be hugely supportive. Taking responsibility for yourself, ditching the victim mentality and learning to love a little bit of routine will go a long way. Making friends with a more methodical approach to life and imposing some structure will support your soul's growth.

Mindful mantras

- Boundaries are a healthy expression of my self-worth

- Asserting boundaries does not make me unlovable

- Creativity and structure are not mutually exclusive

- Access to my heart is a privilege, not a right

Journal prompts

How do I feel when I say 'no' to someone I love? How do the people I love react when I say 'no'?

When do I feel weighed down by my commitments to show up for other people?

What relationships help me feel a sense of stability?

What physical exercises or activities help me feel connected to my body and grounded in reality?

What aspects of my life feel out of control or lacking direction? How could routine support these realms?

The North Node in *Libra* and the South Node in *Aries*

Energetic axis cooperation vs. conflict

Keywords diplomacy, compromise, empathy

Major life lessons

○ Mastering the art of collaboration

○ Approaching life from a place of compromise rather than domination

○ Learning to respond rather than react

○ Finding healthy outlets for anger and aggression

Where you've come from the Aries South Node

The Aries South Node reflects a karmic path rooted in determination, aggression and independence. A desire to dominate shaped your experiences, bringing a distinctly adversarial quality to your life. 'Act now, think later' was your MO; playing to win, staking your claim and stepping forward in the face of danger were instinctive responses.

In this lifetime, it can manifest as being overly competitive or having a tendency to act before you think. Impulsivity, anger and difficulty compromising could cause problems in your relationships. Conflict, confrontation and drama might seem to follow you, or you may struggle to work as part of a team. A tendency to get bored of situations (or people!) could also be a recurring issue.

What you've come here to learn the Libra North Node

The Libra North Node is an invitation to refine your diplomacy skills. This lifetime is all about learning the art of compromise, collaboration and cooperation. Dealing strategically with different personality types and learning the art of negotiation will be difficult but rewarding. Mindful speech will be an important capability to refine. Slowing down, becoming more sensitive to what's going on around you – both socially and in your environment – is also key. Strengthening your empathy muscle and learning to listen and see things from other people's perspectives will unlock opportunities if you're willing to put in the hard work.

Mindful mantras

- ○ Life is a team sport
- ○ Active listening is a superpower
- ○ Collaboration is the key to my success
- ○ I can achieve twice as much when I work with other people

---

Journal prompts

When do I struggle to collaborate with other people?

What is my reaction to being told 'no'?

What experiences or environments am I exposed to that open me up to other people's perspectives?

When do I have the opportunity to improve my skills as a team player?

What happens when I experiment with pausing and responding rather than reacting in conflict?

The North Node in *Scorpio* and the South Node in *Taurus*

Energetic axis intensity vs. security

Keywords focus, shadow, depth

Major life lessons

- Engaging with life on a deeper and more meaningful level

- Taking a proactive approach to healing old wounds

- Exploring your shadow

- Resisting the temptation to play it safe

Where you've come from the Taurus South Node

The Taurus South Node speaks to a karmic path of playing it safe. You rarely (if ever) rocked the boat, and if things felt painful or difficult, you refused to dig deeper to see what was really going on. Maintaining a level of comfort – materially and emotionally – came at the cost of experiencing life to its fullest.

In this lifetime, it can manifest as a tendency to be overly cautious. You may be extra-conservative when it comes to cash or resist any kind of change or disruption to your routine. When things go wrong, you could go to great lengths to avoid examining the root of the problem, preferring to smooth things over and focus on the material here and now.

What you've come here to learn the Scorpio North Node

The North Node in Scorpio is all about intensity, focus and truth. In this lifetime, your soul has incarnated to feel things on a deep, visceral level. This energy is about experiencing life to its fullest and taking a few risks. Rather than keeping things pleasant, this North Node asks you to acknowledge your shadow. Who are you when no one is watching? What wounds are you carrying and what do they need in order to truly heal? This North Node gives you the green light to immerse yourself in something completely rather than just skimming the surface. Giving yourself permission to dive deep into life – whether it's hobbies or relationships – is essential; this is an energy that will thrive when given a sharp focus. Find something to sink your teeth into, and don't hold back.

Mindful mantras

- Playing it safe keeps me playing small

- I am here to experience life in its fullest expression

- I thrive on opportunities to focus and dive deep into experiences

- I cannot heal and release what I refuse to confront

Journal prompts

When do I tend to 'play it safe'?

What interests or areas of life am I intrigued yet terrified by?

How often do I make space to immerse myself in something wholeheartedly?

In what areas of my life do I actively avoid digging beneath the surface?

What emotional wounds am I afraid to acknowledge and deal with?

The North Node in *Sagittarius* and the South Node in *Gemini*

Energetic axis conviction vs. indecision

Keywords faith, adventure, expansion

Major life lessons

- O Exploring life on your own terms

- O Drawing your own conclusions

- O Standing by your opinions

- O Finding connection to something bigger

Where you've come from the Gemini South Node

The Gemini South Node speaks to a karmic path where indecision, anxiety and a lack of focus shaped your previous experiences. You may have struggled with concentration or found yourself swept away in white noise. There was a restlessness to your experience where you struggled to steady yourself, and possibly ran yourself ragged trying to do lots of different things without being able to follow through.

In this lifetime, this signature can manifest as indecisiveness. You may suffer from anxiety, run on a base line of nervous energy or find it difficult to switch off. You could experience difficulties with focus and be avoidant – especially with anything serious or emotional. A hesitancy to commit to things could make you prone to flakiness.

What you've come here to learn the Sagittarius North Node

The North Node in Sagittarius is all about finding the deeper wisdom in your human experience. It's about disconnecting from the chatter of the crowd and letting yourself connect with something meaningful. Allowing yourself the freedom to explore things in your own time, so you can come to your own conclusions and develop your own opinions, will be a salve for your soul. Your challenge is to resist going along with the crowd and to become your own guru. Where do you derive a sense of depth and meaning in life? What are you truly passionate about? Finding the things that make you feel closer to something more meaningful is key.

Mindful mantras

- My journey is my own. I walk my own path

- I trust my instinct and have faith in my opinions

- I am surrounded by divine inspiration on a daily basis

- Standing up for what I believe in is an act of courage

Journal prompts

When do I feel most confident in my own conviction?

When am I most likely swayed by other people's opinions?

What have I started but always regretted not finishing?

What part of the world have I always dreamt of exploring?

The North Node in *Capricorn* and the South Node in *Cancer*

Energetic axis structure vs. receptivity

Keywords patience, grit, ambition

Major life lessons

○ Embracing and owning personal ambitions

○ Nurturing resilience

○ Learning to do things independently

○ Establishing and maintaining healthy boundaries

Where you've come from the Cancer South Node

The South Node in Cancer reflects a karmic path defined by toxic compassion. You may have faced obstacles that meant you could never embrace 'main character energy'. An inability to go after what you truly desired may have left you feeling resentful, as if you never had the space or power to fully realise your potential. In this lifetime you might be prone to using other people's needs as an excuse not to chase your own dreams. Being overwhelmed by external expectations, especially from family, is a real threat. You may have a tendency to hang back and wait for other people to act rather than forging your own path. You may also feel disappointed that no one shows up for you to the same extent as you do for them.

What you've come here to learn the Capricorn North Node

The North Node in Capricorn is all about developing an inner well of resilience and focus. It's about digging your heels in, being brave enough to admit what you really want, and going for it, full tilt. Giving yourself permission to pursue things with everything you've got – and not needing anyone to come along for the ride. Becoming more comfortable with solitude and developing a strong relationship with discipline will be essential. Loving and respecting your family, but not letting yourself be overwhelmed by responsibilities or expectations will be a difficult but worthy exercise. Accepting that the seeds you plant today won't bear fruit tomorrow … but when they do eventually blossom, it will be worth the wait.

Mindful mantras

- I am the boss of my own destiny

- Discipline is an act of self-respect

- I deserve a seat at the table

- Slow and steady wins the race

- I have the power and strength to go after what I want, alone

Journal prompts

In what areas of my life do I let my goals take a backseat in favour of someone else's needs?

In what areas of my life would I like to develop greater discipline?

What areas of life am I afraid to tackle alone?

When do I use other people's feelings as an excuse not to prioritise my own needs?

How do my family's expectations shape the way I move through the world?

The North Node in *Aquarius* and the South Node in *Leo*

Energetic axis rebellion vs. approval

Key words independence, foresight, freedom

Major life lessons

- ◯ Letting your freak flag fly

- ◯ Leading with your head

- ◯ Thinking about the broader impact of your actions

- ◯ Leaving a legacy

Where you've come from the Leo South Node

A Leo South Node reflects karmic baggage of being overly reliant on the praise and acceptance of other people. You may have held a position where popularity, fame or admiration were your greatest measures of success. In this lifetime it can manifest as a deep sensitivity to what other people think of you. A pathological need to be admired, or a tendency to consistently place yourself at the centre of attention could be recurrent themes. You may tend to be self-involved, rather than thinking through and considering how your words and actions might impact other people.

What you've come here to learn the Aquarius North Node

The Aquarius North Node is an invitation to zoom out from your own POV and deepen your appreciation for your place in the universe. Getting comfortable with the smallness and the enormity of it all. Exploring the notion that we are a speck in time, but also that you have the power to make a real mark and effect change. It's a need to connect with what truly matters to you. It's also a deep need to question everything, and not take things on face value, to challenge the status quo and become more self-sufficient. Embracing your quirks and letting them shine – even if they aren't fashionable. Finding a place in community with like-minded souls is also important, as is developing a decision-making style that considers the impact of your actions on both a micro and macro scale.

Mindful mantras

- I am a tiny but powerful part of the universe

- My individuality is my superpower

- I have the power to make a difference

- I am proud of my principles

- My worthiness as a person is not contingent on the amount of attention I receive

---

Journal prompts

What issues or causes truly matter to me?

In what communities or environments do I feel a sense of camaraderie?

How rationally do I think things through before I make a decision?

What environments or activities help me maintain a sense of perspective?

How do I feel when I step back and let other people take up space?

The North Node in *Pisces* and the South Node in *Virgo*

Energetic axis wonder vs. practicality

Key words creativity, fluidity, non-attachment

Major life lessons

○ Loosening your attachment to outcomes

○ Exploring and expressing your creativity

○ Getting out of your head and into your heart

○ Deepening your sense of faith and learning to let go and surrender

Where you've come from the Virgo South Node

The Virgo South Node reflects a karmic path punctuated by an obsessive need to refine, reorganise and improve. Attaining perfection was your MO ... to the extreme. Difficulty resting or allowing things to 'just be' kept you perpetually busy and running on empty.

In this lifetime, it can manifest as a proclivity towards anxiety. You may worry about the worst-case scenario and prepare back-up plans for every possible outcome. A nervous energy that sees you reorganise things even when they're perfectly fine as they are could be a coping mechanism. The quest for improvement can also manifest as body image issues or an unhealthy preoccupation with wellness.

What you've come here to learn the Pisces North Node

The North Node in Pisces is an invitation to slow down and go with the flow. It's a cosmic calling to approach things from a place of creativity rather than critique. Your challenge is to try to be present for what's going on, and notice how people, environments and experiences make you feel, rather than trying to analyse every situation. Learning to lead from your heart rather than your head will be an ongoing process. Letting go of your attachment to how things turn out will support your soul's development. Seeking a deeper sense of wisdom and spiritual significance from your life rather than trying to tick off to-do lists will help you forge new paths.

Mindful mantras

○ Creativity is my life flow

○ I embrace the process rather than chasing the outcome

○ I trust in divine timing

○ Order does not equal happiness

○ Good enough is good enough

Journal prompts

When do I let myself colour outside the lines?

In what areas of my life do I feel most creatively in flow?

Where do I feel driven by a need to attain perfection?

How does it feel when I engage in creativity for the sake of it (not to achieve a desired outcome)?

What activities or practices help me feel a sense of connection to something greater?

Acknowledgements

Thank you to my mother, Donna, for instilling a love of words – and astrology – from an early age. Your love and encouragement throughout this project (and my whole life!) means everything. To my brother, Adam, for nurturing a love of books, music and of course, Aquarians! To my father, Chum, for making spirituality a completely normal part of daily life. I wish you were here to see this, but I have no doubt you're toasting me with a ginger beer on the other side.

To my first astrology teacher Marc Laurenson, and Sydney Astrology School. Thank you for guiding me on this path and embodying all that is empowering and inspiring about this craft. To Kelly Surtees, I am forever grateful for your kindness, wisdom and encouragement.

To Jean Marie for believing I had a book in me and opening the door for this project to take shape. You're the best!

To my editor Vicky for your patience and skill. To Antonietta for being the calmest, most capable project manager ever. So grateful for your Capricorn/Gemini smarts. To Alice for backing me and believing this book could be something truly special. To Murray for your insurmountable patience and creative vision. Thank you for making it look so beautiful.

To Rachel for being my most vocal supporter and making me feel like no dilemma is ever too small (or neurotic) to work through. Your faith in me and encouragement of this project has been pivotal to my persistence.

To Lisa, thank you for your eagle eyes and sixth sense which ensures you always know the perfect time to call. To Charlie for being my unofficial hype girl and for listening and loving me without judgement. To Kath for being there no matter what; forever and always, I'd take the low shelf for you. To AP, Peemy and Acc, for knowing that words of affirmation are my preferred love language. Our WhatsApp threads have been a lifeline throughout this project. Thank you.

To my dream readers Rosy and Mags. Your ongoing advice on everything from structure, to cover design has been incredible. I am so lucky to call you family as well as friends. I really hope you love the finished product.

To Mary and Guy – this book would literally not exist without you. Thank you for giving me the gift of time and space to make this dream a reality and being the best grandparents and friends imaginable.

To my old souls Plum and Sid, I can't quite believe how patient and understanding you have been while I was glued to a computer for months on end. You are living proof of the delight and fulfilment that comes when we follow the North Node path. Being your mum is my favourite gig ever.

And finally to Matt. Your belief in me leaves me speechless. No goal too crazy, no practice too esoteric. I literally have no words, just eternal gratitude. I must have done something really good in a past life to find you in this one. I love you!

About the author

Emma Vidgen is an Australian astrologer, meditation teacher and journalist. Her fascination with the stars began as a child, despite being chastised for being the 'world's most untidy Virgo'. Emma is passionate about making esoteric practices accessible and fun. She loves to weave music, fashion and pop culture into conversations about life, death and everything in between. She is obsessed with vintage shopping and hot sauce and would like to be reincarnated as a professional musician. She lives in Sydney with her Libran daughter, Capricorn son, Sagittarian husband and Scorpio AF cat.

Scan the QR code to download free worksheet
PDFs designed to accompany this book.

Published in 2022 by Hardie Grant Books, an imprint of Hardie Grant Publishing

Hardie Grant Books (Melbourne)
Wurundjeri Country
Building 1, 658 Church Street
Richmond, Victoria 3121

Hardie Grant Books (London)
5th & 6th Floors
52–54 Southwark Street
London SE1 1UN

hardiegrantbooks.com

Hardie Grant acknowledges the Traditional Owners of the country on which we work, the Wurundjeri people of the Kulin nation and the Gadigal people of the Eora nation, and recognises their continuing connection to the land, waters and culture. We pay our respects to their Elders past and present.

A catalogue record for this book is available from the National Library of Australia

References to Steven Forrest (http://www.forrestastrology.com) and Forrest Center for Evolutionary Astrology (http://www.forrestastrology.center) appear with permission from Steven Forrest ©

All charts in this book were calculated using Astro Gold for macOS, by Esoteric Technologies www.esotech.com.au

Every effort has been made to trace, contact and acknowledge all copyright holders. Please contact the publisher with any information on errors or omissions.

The Astrology of You
ISBN 978 1 74379 800 3
10 9 8 7 6 5 4 3 2 1

Publisher: Alice Hardie-Grant
Project Editor: Antonietta Melideo
Editor: Victoria Fisher
Design Manager: Kristin Thomas
Designer: Murray Batten
Production Manager: Todd Rechner

Colour reproduction by Splitting Image Colour Studio
Printed in China by Leo Paper Products LTD.